THE LAKE GODDESS

The Lake GODDESS

Flora Nwapa

Abibiman Publishing
New York & London

First published in the United Kingdom in 2023 by
Abibiman Publishing.
www.abibimanpublishing.com

First published in Nigeria in 2020 by Tana Press Ltd.

First published as an e-book in 2019 by
Tana Press with the support of Digitalback Books and Worldreader.

Copyright © 2023 Flora Nwapa.

All rights reserved. No part of this book may be reproduced, stored in a retrieval system, or transmitted in any form or by any means without permission in writing from the publisher.

Abibiman Publishing is registered under
Hudics LLC in the United States and in the United Kingdom.

ISBN: 978-1-7392767-0-6

This is a work of fiction. Names, characters, places, and incidents either are the product of the author's imagination or are used fictitiously. Any resemblance to actual persons, living or dead, events, or locales is entirely coincidental.

Cover design by Stephen Embleton

Printed in the United Kingdom by Clays Ltd.

Introduction to the 2023 Edition

"Ogbuide wants every woman to have a voice."

It has been a privilege to work with Flora Nwapa's family — her three children, Ejine Nzeribe, Amede Nzeribe, and Uzoma Nwakuche — and seeing their commitment to their mother's legacy, ensuring it is kept alive in a world, which will always yearn for the magic of Ogbuide, The Lake Goddess. ***The Lake Goddess*** is a testament to the power of traditions, beliefs and heritage, in a world quick to minimise the importance of cosmologies, of the eons of ancestors trying to make sense of the world around them, and calling on something greater than themselves for guidance.

I wanted to have an understanding of who Flora Nwapa was, and continues to be, for three individuals who have remained steadfast custodians of their mother's work, and in particular, the bold task of having posthumously published ***The Lake Goddess*** in 2019, decades after her passing. Thirty years is a long time, but just below the surface reside the memories of their lives together, hints at where Flora Nwapa was in her own life when she wrapped up the manuscript for *The Lake Goddess,* and the day-to-day lives not often spoken of, when ***The Lake Goddess*** is very much that – the day-to-day lives of a community rationalising the old and the new. For Ejine and I, our first face-to-face meeting in

Lagos in 2022 was an emotional one: speaking of mothers and who they are to us, being brought up by them and growing up to see who they are in our world, and to the rest of the world. Ejine shared the turmoil of the political climate as a girl and her profound experiences of her mother, and remarkably, the direct experience of The Lake Goddess herself when forced to leave their old lives and home behind. And we are indebted to Obioma Nnaemeka, who edited the version that we are publishing.

As the first woman published under the original African Writers Series, Flora Nwapa's *Efuru* was bold in its approach and representation of her world and worldview. To me, **The Lake Goddess** is even bolder. It was a pleasant surprise to read the connection to *Efuru* within the narrative, tying her first novel to her final work. Flora Nwapa's characters face the world head on and express their views, with few grey areas. They argue, as I imagine Flora Nwapa did within herself, or in conversations with others, for a changing world to better understand how they function on tradition versus new ideas, and the strength in the feminine aspect of society and beliefs, revealing a deeper thread of higher power within us all.

Stephen Embleton
Editor
Oxford, December 2022

Preface

IN THE END IS THE BEGINNING

Flora Nwapa's *The Lake Goddess* is the admirable and enthralling apotheosis of the various poignant colors of her feministic ideology. It brings together her understanding and projection of woman. In this novel, she presents her true feministic vision in a more composite form, pulling ideas and sub-themes of womanhood together, and drawing from her major novels of *Efuru* (1966), *Idu* (1970), *One is Enough* (1981), *Women are Different* (1986), and her play, *Conversations* (1993). She coalesced them in *The Lake Goddess* (2017).

She weaves the women's tapestry in the domestic setting of the family in the ambience of her beloved Oguta environment, with the beautiful lake abode of the goddess. Central to her ideology of womanhood is the Lake Goddess, Ogbuide, Uhamiri, an independent deity, even in such a predominantly masculine realm of gods and spirits, who holds her own with beauty, majesty and grandeur. In projecting the character of the Lake Goddess, she posits her ideology of female empowerment with this goddess prototype. Ogbuide is Nwapa's answer and panacea to a worthy, fulfilling life.

In Ogbuide, Nwapa constructed and defined, in graphic details, the cult of womanhood. This is beyond the mortal realm; it stems from the supernatural and permeates the natural world. The cult of womanhood is the cult of life essence, symbolized in water. The Lake Goddess, in her watery queendom, is eulogized as Ogbuide, Uhamiri, and Ezemiri:

> Protector of women
> Life is water
> Mother and water are the same
> Without water, who can live?
> Without mother, who can live?
> (251)

Uhamiri is "mother of all mothers," (238), and "owner of the lake, owner of the fishes, owner of the people" (238). She is the anchor of women and their enabler.

An important feature of this book is Nwapa's endemic culturalism which imbues her writing and episteme with relevance and vigor. She accosts the hydra-headed conflict of Christianity and Oguta Traditional

Religion. Here she makes a powerful statement of returning to our roots. She leads the reader on through the paths of first, the traditional religion, divination and medical practice in the character of Mgbada's father.

Then, she posits Mgbada, the son, in the annals of the Christian religion and education and a teaching profession. Nwapa introduces hybridity, as a compromise. However, later in the futility of the project, she situates Mgbada squarely as a true son of his father, who inherited the mantle of Oguta cultural practices and gleefully preserves them. She does the same with Ona, Ogbuide's neophyte, who is repulsed by both Christianity and its Missionary Education. Ultimately, Ona even gives up wifehood and motherhood to become Ogbuide's priestess. Such is Nwapa's strong statement on the need to preserve our indigenous African religion and culture.

Nwapa believes in the emancipation of the human spirit and its dynamism in introducing change. Thus, she combats women's issues still within the ambience of culture. In this novel, therefore, Nwapa undertakes the great task of showing women how to break the shackles of hurtful and subsuming, traditional practices, such as female circumcision. Teach ably, this was done by the women themselves, thereby upgrading her stance in the situation of *Efuru* in her eponymous novel.

In *The Lake Goddess*, Nwapa continued with her

mantra of marriage and motherhood with forceful emphasis. She, however, introduces a powerful proposition to aid women in navigating the turbulent waters of matrimony.

Polygamy, the folly of many wives, debases women in their questing and competing for the love of their husband. She introduces the notion of choice for women: "A woman should marry once in her lifetime unless she wants children which her present husband fails to provide" (132). This echoes an incident in her novel *Idu*. She continues, "Women should marry but we should not make our husbands little gods; we pet them too much and they are like little children" (132). The above precepts are Nwapa's advice to women to forge an identity of self. She emphasizes education and employment, as means of gaining financial viability.

There is an adage that poverty is the face of women. Nwapa takes it further and writes, "Woman's other name is suffering" (13). She presents education as the gateway to financial viability and poverty's mitigation. In this novel, Nwapa lays bare all her ideas on women's emancipation but significantly, she stresses that this lies with the women themselves. This posits the individuation of women's elevation. Like Ogbuide, the Lake Goddess, her prototype, woman must seek her upliftment within her cultural space and buttress it with hard work, sisterhood, bonding, and sustainability. Women should not be voiceless. Like water, women must maintain their rightful place in society for communal growth.

In *The Lake Goddess*, Nwapa leaves her testament and manifesto for posterity, for here she bares her soul. Flora Nwapa still lives in her works, and we hear her still.

Professor Helen Chukwuma
Department of English and Modern
Foreign Languages
Jackson State University
Jackson, Mississippi

Introduction

THE LAKE GODDESS MATTERS!

"It doesn't matter where we worship or what we call God, there is only one, interdependent human family."[1]
—**Archbishop Emeritus Desmond Tutu,**
1984 Nobel Peace Prize Laureate

"Great Goddess/The Supreme God/Made you great/ By making you/The Water Goddess/ I must be your Priestess/Until I die"[2]
—**Flora Nwapa**, *The Lake Goddess* (1992)

Gods are predominantly featured as males in the religious pantheon throughout the world. However, Flora Nwapa projects a female goddess, called Ogbuide, in her novel, *The Lake Goddess*. In demonstrating female sovereignty in the spiritual realm in her hometown, Oguta, Flora Nwapa establishes the ascendancy and empowerment of the water deity, Ogbuide. In the wake of many religions, in Nigeria, thwarting the supremacy of this rich and powerful Water Monarch, aka, Ezemiri, Flora Nwapa establishes the Oguta indigenous community's respect for their roots, and worship of the water deity, popularly called Mammywater, throughout Nigeria[3] (Jell-Bahlsen, *Research in African Literatures,* 1995, 30-41).

This mystical "Lady of the Lake," is at the center of Flora Nwapa's creative corpus, i.e., *Efuru, Idu, Never Again, One Is Enough, This Is Lagos and Other Stories, Wives at War and Other Stories, Cassava Song* and *Rice Song, Women are Different,* her children's book, *Mammywater,* and her plays, *Conversations* and *The First Lady.* The Lake Goddess is symbolic of economic independence for women, female empowerment, and female strength and wisdom.

The novel, *The Lake Goddess,* is a bildungsroman, where the reader follows the life of the protagonist, Ona, from the beginning to the end of the book. In fact, it is the biography of the Priestess of Oguta Lake around 1989-90 in Oguta. Flora Nwapa was conducting interviews and research, for a forthcoming conference at New York Public Library's Schomburg Center for Research in Black Culture. The conference convener, Professor Flora E. S. Kaplan in the Department of Anthropology, at New York University, was on leave in Benin, Nigeria from 1988-1989. She was conducting research on how

African women exercised power, authority, and influence and the subtleties and complexities of the contemporary spheres of power they often share with men[4] (Kaplan 1997, xxxii). She invited Flora Nwapa to the conference to expand the notions of women's power in Oguta.

After Flora Nwapa's field research at Oguta II, where the Priestess of Oguta Lake lives, she presented a paper at the 1991 conference in New York entitled, "Priestesses and Power among the Riverine Igbo," and said:

> Ezemiri wielded tremendous power in her community. She was a diviner, as well as a medicine woman who could cure the sick and the afflicted with water, roots, herbs and incantations. She ministered to whomsoever consulted her from far and near and spoke authoritatively in the name of the Goddess. Invoking the Goddess, the priestess first called on the Supreme God: 'Supreme God/You gave me power/You are water.' Thus, water is the most important item of her cure. She also used white chalk and the feathers of different kinds of birds. She gave her sister's daughter in marriage to her husband, once she entered priesthood. The priestess's powers are derived from

the supernatural.[5] (Kaplan, *Queens, Queen Mothers, Priestesses and Power,* 1997, 419-420).

Upon her return to Nigeria, Flora Nwapa began "writing another book, titled, The Story of A Priestess: A Novel."[6] (Umeh, *A Pen and A Press,* 103). Without a doubt, Ogbuide is Flora Nwapa's muse, who inspired her to write and publish books.

She shares the circumstances in her life that helped her to find her voice:

> As a child I would call on anybody who promised to tell me a story. I would sit down and listen. And when I went to high school I had read practically everything that I could find... Having written *Efuru* and published it, I continued to write. Now when I had my own publishing company, I decided that I needed books for my growing children... I started writing children's books. I wrote *Mammywater* in 1979[7] (Umeh, 1995, 25).

In Nwapa's last novel, the author demonstrates the ultimate power of Ogbuide. Ona, a priestess, chosen by Ogbuide upon her birth, is empowered with the gift of prophecy, healing and wish fulfillment, as she conducts her rituals for her worshippers, and communicates with Ogbuide. The conflict elevates as Ona's Christian parents, Mgbada and Akpe, reject the call of Ezemiri, and subsequently send their daughter to a local missionary school. When they fail to initiate her into the church, they approve her marriage to Mr. Sylvester Chukwukere, a successful, travelling pharmaceutical salesman, with the hope of breaking her attachment to the Water Monarch, Ezemiri.

Every society has belief systems which teach the community its spiritual values. However, advocates of Christianity failed to recognize the humanity in indigenous religions. Their intolerance for African spirituality was the bedrock for British colonial's subsequent subjugation of Nigerians and their culture in myriad ways. Flora Nwapa's double voice censures foreign religious aggression at the beginning of her novel, *The Lake Goddess*:

> ... [W]hen Mgbada was ten years old, a strange thing happened in the town of Ugwuta. Strange people came to the town with strange ideas. They talked of a god who was born by a woman and who died for the sins of the world. They criticized the religion of the people, calling them pagans and heathens... Mgbada's father was upset by this new religion. He protested

> thus: 'What kind of religion preached that one should abandon the worship of one's ancestors...' So, before he died, he charged Mgbada: 'Whatever you do, whatever you become, don't forget the worship of our ancestors...'[8] (6-7).

In *The Lake Goddess*, Nwapa questions Christian missionary dogma and she advocates for the return to Oguta traditional cosmology. As Chimalum Nwankwo points this out in his essay, "*The Lake Goddess:* The Roots of Nwapa's Word":

> In this novel, tradition suffers incursion but survives by a clear authorial privileging that surpasses the political engagement of previous works. The Lake Goddess remains in the center of all this, and that Ona triumphs is an expression which calls for and affirms a continuity of traditional values stretching from Mgbada's father, through Mgbada, to the fictional present. The situation responds to the widely accepted perception of tradition as a continuum is that well-known essay by T. S. Eliot, *Tradition and the Individual Talent*[9] (345).

Nwapa adapts a new voice in *The Lake Goddess*. Her womanist politics go beyond challenging female representation in Nigerian letters by male authors. Her critique of British religious imperialism—by censuring Christian missionary education's intolerance of indigenous Oguta religion—presents a new voice from this gifted author of the biographies of Oguta women and men. Zadie Smith, in her essay, *Speaking in Tongues*, contends that "Voices are meant to be unchanging and singular... We feel that our voices are who we are and that to have more than one or to use different versions of a voice for different occasions, represents, at best, a Janus-faced duplicity, and at worst, the loss of our very souls"[10] (2).

Flora Nwapa's adoption of another voice establishes the fact that she has made peace with her paternal grandparents, who practiced ancestor worship, to the chagrin of her Christian peers who would accuse her of class and religious betrayal. The anthropologist, Sabine Jell-Bahlsen, in her chapter, *Ogbuide's Famous Daughter, Flora Nwapa*, in her book, *The Water Goddess in Igbo Cosmology, Ogbuide of Oguta Lake* has the last word: "Nwapa's attitude towards her own culture was dynamic and her views on local beliefs and their significance for women have changed throughout her life and *oeuvre*"[11](385).

Flora Nwapa demonstrates Ona's spiritual power

in one of her rituals as she invokes the Lake Goddess to answer the prayers of the fish-sellers, Ekecha and Mgbeke:

> Beautiful woman/Hairy woman/Ageless woman/Mother of all mothers/Owner of the Lake/Owner of the fishes/Owner of the People/Of the Lake/Protector of the Lake People/Ogbuide/ Ohamiri/ Ezemiri/Queen Mother/Goddesss of the Water/Goddess of the fishes/The Goddess of thunder/ The Goddess of lightning/The protector of women/The Lake Goddess/Your priestess/ Salutes you/Your fellow women/
>
> Salute you/They are here before you/ So come to their help/I beseech you/ Good Mother/Give them/Your abundant/ Blessings/ Show them the light'[12] (238-9).

Ogbuide is the custodian of Oguta land and its people, as indicated in the praise song. When the Europeans, especially the Portuguese and the British, came across the lake and commenced trade with the Oguta people in the 18th century, the revered Lake Goddess was already esteemed as a source of consolation, strength, nourishment, wellbeing, protection, and wealth to the people in and around the lake area[13] (Umeh, *A Pen and*

A Press, 7). By the end of the novel, Mgbada's relations, especially his son-in-law, finally accept the will of the Water Monarch, after much family discord, constant confusion and painful decisions. They finally realize that Ona belongs to the Lake Goddess, Uhamiri. As a result, she must end her marriage to her husband, Mr. Sylvester Chukwukere. Ona, according to Oguta traditions, moves back to her father's compound, rents a stall at Oguta market, and pursues her innate profession as the priestess of the Lake Goddess, Ogbuide, in spite of her husband's cry, 'The Spirit has killed me'[14a] (223). Mgbada responds with compassion and love to his distressed in-law with an age-old proverb, 'When the gods give us craw-craw, they also give us nails with which to scratch'[14b] (223.) He enlightens all his family members about the *modus vivendi* of the Oguta people. He also keeps Ona's family together by finding a second wife for Mr. Sylvester in the Oguta vicinity. In this way, he would be closer to his three children to nurture them. This is a very wise decision under the circumstances. When Mr. Sylvester's kith and kin learned that their son was married to a water spirit, they advised him to return home, which he refused to do.

The 1984 Nobel Laureate for Peace, Archbishop Desmond Tutu says, "Religion is about the manner in which we interact with others, and our broader responsibilities to the human family and the earth we share"[15] (14). Even though African men wield a great deal of power in Igbo society, African women are also symbiotic power brokers. Flora Nwapa, in her portrayal of the Priestess of Ogbuide, who dwells at the bottom of Oguta's beautiful, clear blue lake, insists on the complementary nature of Oguta society, beginning with a mixed-gender and age-grade system, a mystical Lake Goddess, who is partial to women, but guarantees women, as well as men, peace, power, prominence, and prosperity.

Dr. Marie Linton Umeh, CUNY,
President, Flora Nwapa Society International,
Ambassador, UN/UNESCO African Women for Good Governance,
UN Representative,
Widows Development Organisation (WiDO).

Notes

1. Desmond Tutu: "God Is Not A Christian. Nor a Jew, Muslim, Hindu…" by Grant Schreiber, May 29, 2015. https://real-leaders.com/desmond-tutu-god-is-not-a-christian-nor-a-jew-muslim-hindu/
2. Flora Nwapa, *The Lake Goddess*. Bookbaby. Kindle. !st Edition. July 16, 2020.
3. Sabine Jell-Bahlsen. "The Concept of Mammywater in Flora Nwapa's Novels." *Research in African Literatures*. 26:2 (Summer 1995):30-41.
4. Flora E. S. Kaplan. *Queens, Queen Mothers, Priestesses and Power: Case Studies in African Gender*. New York: The New York Academy of Sciences. 1997, xxxii.
5. Flora Nwapa. "Priestesses and Power among The Riverine Igbo." In Flora E. S. Kaplan, *Queens, Queen Mothers. Priestesses and Power: Case Studies in African Gender*. New York: The New York Academy of Sciences. 1997, 415-424.
6. Marie Umeh. *Flora Nwapa: A Pen and A Press*. New York: Triatlantic Books of NY. 2010, 103.
7. Marie Umeh. "The Poetics of Economic Independence for Female Empowerment: An Inter view with Flora Nwapa." *Research in African Literatures*. 26.2 (Summer 1995):22-29.
8. Flora Nwapa, *The Lake Goddess*, 6-7.
9. Chimalum Nwankwo. "*The Lake Goddess*: The

Roots of Nwapa's Word." In Marie Umeh. *Emerging Perspectives on Flora Nwapa: Critical and Theoretical Essays*. Trenton, NJ: Africa World Press. 1998, 335-352.

10. Zadie Smith. "Speaking in Tongues." *The New York Review of Books*. Feb. 26, 2009, 1-6.
11. Sabine Jell-Bahlsen. *The Water Goddess in Igbo Cosmology. Ogbuide of Oguta Lake*. Trenton, NJ. Africa World Press. 1998, 385.
12. Flora Nwapa, *The Lake Goddess*, 238-9.
13. M. Umeh. *Flora Nwapa: A Pen and A Press*, 7.
14. Flora Nwapa. *The Lake Goddess*, 223.
15. Desmond Tutu: "God Is Not A Christian, Nor a Jew, Muslim, Hindu. . . ." by Grant Schreiber, May 29, 2015. https://real-leaders.com/desmond-tutu-God-is-not-a-christian-nor-a-jew-muslim-hindu/

Chapter 1

Mgbada was the first son of his father who was a medicine man and a diviner. Tradition demanded that he would inherit his father's skills. So, as early as five years old, he had begun to carry his father's bag and to learn from him about the roots, leaves and different kinds of herbs for traditional healing.

Mgbada learnt fast. He knew the names of different plants. He knew those that were edible and those that were poisonous. He learnt how to prepare them and what ailments they were used for.

When his father sacrificed to the ancestors, Mgbada was present. He learnt the incantations, the praise names used and the mode of the sacrifices.

Outside the home, Mgbada followed his age-grade to fish in the Lake, the river and the stream. He became a good fisherman, and he knew where to catch different kinds of fish during different seasons of the year. Everybody said that he was the true son of his father.

His father said aloud to anybody who cared to listen that he was happy with his son, and that when the end came, he would dance to the abode of the ancestors for he had left what they bequeathed to him in competent hands.

Then when Mgbada was ten years old, a strange thing happened in the town of Ugwuta. Strange people came to the town with strange ideas. They talked of a god who was born by a woman and who died for the sins of the world. They criticized the religion of the people, calling them pagans and heathens. On certain days of the week, they congregated, they prayed and sang all day.

Mgbada's father was upset by this new religion. He protested thus:

"What kind of religion preached that one should abandon the worship of one's ancestors? Why should these people who were foreigners for that matter be concerned about where one went when one died? We know that there is life after death and so when we die, we join our ancestors and continue to live."

But his protests were too late; his own brother and his mother had joined the new religion. He held on to Mgbada and virtually begged him to uphold his heritage. Mgbada held on, but pressure was from all sides. Those who embraced the new religion were becoming distinguished. Mgbada's father knew that he was losing his grip on his first son and so before he died, he charged Mgbada thus:

"Whatever you do, whatever you become, don't forget the worship of our ancestors. You have the *ofo* of our family. You are the first son. Much is expected of you. You must carry on after me."

So, after his father's death, Mgbada at the age of eleven went to school, and was baptized as Joseph. But he did not like school very much. The influence of his mother was too great. He went to school and church and at the same time worshipped his ancestors. The fact that others abandoned their religion did not make any impression on him. Mgbada carried on in school; he passed his examinations and at the age of seventeen he obtained his first school leaving certificate. With the help of his mother and his uncle who were great influences in the church, he went to a teachers' training college where he spent four years. He returned home and began his career as a teacher. He could easily have been the headmaster of the school, but he preferred to be an ordinary teacher so that he could find time to practice his other profession. He did well. People came to him to cure little ailments. Women, who wanted to sacrifice to their ancestors, came to him with their cocks and hens. The members of the church grumbled, but the priest, eager to have more converts, did not react the way that was expected.

When Mgbada was twenty-three years old, he told his mother that he needed a wife. His mother replied:

"You need a wife, my son, have you found one?"

"Yes."

"Who is she?"

"The daughter of Okoronkwo of Umuikwu Village."

"The daughter of my namesake?" His mother asked, for her name was also Theresa.

"Mama Theresa's daughter."

"Maria?"

"Maria, but I call her Akpe."

"Akpe, that's good. You have chosen well, my son. Have you talked to her?"

Mgbada smiled. "I have written letters to her."

"She likes us?"

"She does."

"What are we waiting for?"

Mgbada was silent. Then he said: "I want to send her to a convent."

"Convent?"

"To learn; to be trained."

"Her mother did not train her?"

Mgbada was silent again.

"How long will this take?"

"Four years."

"You are joking. How old is she?"

"About my age."

"She is a woman. She went to school. She can read and write. Can she sew?"

"She is learning to sew now."

"What are we waiting for? She will learn the rest on the job."

Two days later, Mgbada's mother, Nwafor, went to see Akpe's mother.

"Mama Theresa, good morning, ma."

"Akpe, my daughter, good morning. Is your mother at home?"

"She is at home, ma. Sit down, ma, while I call her. Here is a chair."

Nwafor sat down and looked around her, and was satisfied with what she saw.

"I think we have made a good choice. The house is clean, Akpe has received me well. She is already trained. There is no point going to a convent. All that waste of money and time…" she thought.

"Theresa, welcome. As you have come to us today, is it well?"

"Theresa, my namesake, how are you? I did not see you at mass this morning. So, I thought I should come and find out whether all is well with you and your household."

"Very kind of my namesake to notice that I was not at morning mass. You know I never miss morning mass. My usual problem."

"Your back?"

"My back. This back is going to take me to the land of the dead."

Nwafor began to laugh at the exaggeration.

"Please don't laugh. It is not a laughing matter. This morning I could not get up from bed. You know I rise at five o'clock, have a cold bath—yes, a cold bath, I never can pour hot water on my body. Then I get ready and go to morning mass. But this morning, it was impossible. I did not want to force myself, so I stayed in bed. When I felt better, I had my bath, and was just dressing up when my daughter told me you were in the sitting room. Welcome my sister. Maria, please bring some kola nuts."

"You are feeling better?"

"Much better, but I have to see the doctor when he comes next month."

"The doctor will come next month?"

"Yes, next month. It was announced in the church last Sunday. You didn't hear?"

"I must have heard, but forgot. My namesake, I forget so easily these days. Do you forget as I do?"

"It is old age."

"What do you mean, old age?"

"We have to accept it graciously, my namesake."

"You are old, not me. I am as young as I wish to be."

"I agree with you, but old age is creeping in and you see… Maria, place the kola nut on the stool. Why are you still holding it? Here is a stool, place it here and bring a knife. Why did you not bring a knife?"

"I am sorry, mother," Akpe apologized.

When she brought the knife, her mother sent her on an errand, for she suspected that Nwafor had come to say something rather important.

"Kola nut has come."

"The king's kola is in the king's hand, so break it," said Nwafor.

"No, my namesake, break the kola. You are in my house; I give you the power to break it. I know that I am older than you are."

"Well, if it is that, I am not going to break the kola. You are not older than me."

"We are in the same age-grade."

"Yes, of course," agreed Mama Theresa. "But that does not mean that you are older than me"

"When were you born?"

"Let's not go into that again. Our mothers settled it before they died. Mother said that she and your mother were pregnant during the New Yam Festival. Their age-grade teased them and made predictions on who would give birth first. I came first. Your mother and father went to Aguleri to buy seed yams; it was when they returned that you were born. Therefore, *abumi okeyi chi*. Nevertheless, break the kola. I give you the power to break it."

Without further ado, Mama Theresa took the kola nut from the dish and said:

She who brings kola brings life
Theresa, my namesake
To your health
You remembered me today
May your visit
Be beneficial to both of us
And to our families
May we prosper in old age
May our children prosper
And to me who brought the kola
My health
To my daughter's health
And to your son's health
In the name of Jesus Christ
Amen.

She broke the kola nut, there were five lobes.

"Who is the great yam farmer?"

The women laughed.

"So, you believe that, too?"

"Don't you?"

"Let's leave it at that."

"The kola is good," Mgbada's mother began to chew with relish.

"I buy good kola nuts," Mama Theresa boasted.

"I can see that. Did you buy it last Nkwo?"

"No. You can't buy this kind of kola nut from

Nkwo. This was bought from Mgbidi. I have a friend who brings kola nuts for me from there every Nkwo. She has lots and lots of kola nut trees on her farm."

"Really? A woman?"

"A woman. A friend of mine. A widow like all of us. She has acres of fruit trees. A good Christian, too. Since the death of her husband, she makes money from the fruit trees. All her children are trained from the proceeds of the farm."

"Lucky woman."

"Lucky woman? There is no luck about it. It is hard work. Here we are contented with very little. We could plant fruit trees in our rich soil. But no, we don't. Our men only plant yams, the king of all crops. They leave cassava and vegetables for the women to cultivate. They should plant cash crops."

They fell silent.

"My namesake, I have *kai kai*. It is rather chilly this morning."

As she spoke, she went in and brought a bottle of *kai kai* and two small glasses. She poured a generous amount into each glass and handed one to her visitor. They both drank in gulps. Mgbada's mother praised the *kai kai*.

"I buy good *kai kai*. I have someone who brings it from Patani."

"Patani, yes, they have good *kai kai* there. So, our women still go there?"

"They do. Our women are industrious. You remember when we were young, we went to such far away markets. The young ones still do."

"We suffered."

"Woman's other name is suffering."

"And if you don't suffer, you will not eat."

"Those who went to school are better off."

"They are. At least they can teach or sew. Then they marry well."

"So, they escape the suffering of paddling down the Great River to such places like Patani, Warri and Forcados to buy and sell."

"My namesake, let's have another round."

They drank again and Mgbada's mother said: "*Kai kai* has a way of attracting people, so put away the bottle…"

Someone coughed.

"Didn't I say?"

"Come in, come in. Is that my neighbor?"

Okonyia came in.

"So, you are in. Sit down and eat kola with us," said Mgbada's mother.

"I don't eat kola."

"Of course. Then drink with us."

"On an empty stomach?"

"*Ewo-o*, my neighbor, I have not cooked. I have *anara*."

"I can eat *anara*."

"Good."

"Nwafor, how are you?" asked Okonyia.

"I am well. You did not go to the farm?"

"Since when?" Mama Theresa added. "Our Okonyia has given up farming two planting seasons ago."

"Is that so?"

"Yes," Okonyia answered. "Somebody is calling me. I will be back."

He then left.

"He said he hadn't eaten."

"He expects me to give him food."

"Do you give him sometimes?"

"I do. What can I do? His wife died. His children have all left home. I have advised him to remarry, but he refused."

"He should. He cannot live like this."

"The children should take care of him. Imagine having children and they are not in a position to be of help to you in old age."

"That's life."

They went on drinking. Okonyia did not come back.

"My namesake, I have had enough, put the bottle away before Ojiuzo comes in."

The two women burst into laughter. Then Mgbada's mother said, "Poor widow."

"What do you mean, poor widow? Aren't we all poor widows?"

"No." Mama Theresa shook her head in understanding. "My namesake, we are all widows, we all have our problems, but this particular woman…" she shook her head sadly.

"I know she lost all her children in infancy."

"Yes, but that is not all. She helped her husband marry a young wife who brought forth two lovely children. She took care of the children as if they were hers. Her husband died; then the young wife died. Then a relation of the young wife took the children to Lagos, and nobody knows where they are. The relation doesn't visit home. You see what I mean? So, the woman spends the little money she has buying *kai kai*. And if you ask her why she drank so much, she would reply that if she did not drink, she could not cope with the day-to-day problem of being alive. Do you blame her?"

Nwafor shook her head in sympathy.

"Some women suffer in this world."

"We should thank our God. We have little, but God has blessed the little we have. Ojiuzo suffered, my namesake. You know her husband used to beat her when he married the young wife."

"And she helped him in marrying the young girl, I learnt."

"She paid the entire bride-wealth, my namesake.

But she did not let anybody know that she did; only her husband knew."

"Is that so?"

"Yes, I know about it."

"Why was he so ungrateful?"

"Male ego. He couldn't live down the truth, that his wife whom he married with his money could have enough money to pay the bride-wealth of his new wife."

"Why didn't he use his own money then?"

"His own money? He had no money."

"So, he resented his wife's generosity?"

"Exactly."

"I don't understand it."

"Neither do I."

They fell silent.

"*Ewo-o*, my namesake, it seems as if one is going to see a ghost in this compound today. Where has everybody gone?"

Nwafor said, "Well, the plight of widows. But I am not complaining. Those who used to visit my husband were unbelievers, anyway. So, no more sacrifices to the ancestors, no more pagan festivities. That's why it is so peaceful."

"You are right, my namesake," Nwafor said. There was no point contradicting Mama Theresa. She knows what she believes in. She is a Christian, but she appreciates some non-Christian traditions.

"Our people are ignorant. Jesus Christ is the only living God."

"You are right."

"And I am not going to allow an unbeliever to marry my daughter."

"Of course not!"

"You agree with me?"

"Of course, I agree with you. Your daughter went to school. Have you ever seen in this town a girl who went to school marry a man who did not go to school?"

"Well then. It is only the educated men who marry illiterate girls."

"That's how it should be," Mama Theresa said, getting up. "Maria is keeping long."

"Don't worry, she will soon come back. Is your back still painful?"

Nwafor asked, noticing how difficult it was for Mama Theresa to get up.

"I have said that this back will take me to the land of the dead."

"God forbid, please don't say that again. Why not see a medicine man before the mission doctor comes next month?"

"I don't believe in medicine men; they are all liars and cheats."

"You can try my son. He is not a liar; he is not a cheat either."

"Your son, Joseph?"

"Yes, Joseph or Mgbada, what does it matter? I call him Mgbada. I am so used to the name his father gave him when he was born."

"You mustn't continue to call him that pagan name, Theresa. You must call him Joseph. Joseph is his Christian name. Drop that pagan name."

"Yes, my namesake, you are right. I should drop it; I must make an effort."

"You must. Now that he is teaching the young in this town, he must show a good example. But is what I hear correct?"

"What did you hear?"

"That he still holds the *ofo*. So, he sacrifices to the ancestors."

"He has no choice; he is the first son." She continued.

"His pagan brother can do that."

"But he is the first son. You want him to give up his heritage as the first son? No, I don't think I will allow that."

"Heritage, worldly things. They are not important."

"Remember the story of Esau and Jacob. How do you read your *Bible*? That's Maria returning," said Nwafor.

She did not want to upset her hostess by calling the girl by her traditional name.

"Maria, did you see Rosa?" asked Mama Theresa.

"She was not in. So, I waited for her but she did not return. I thought I was wasting too much time, so I came back."

"Good girl. Now go back there. I am sure that she has come back by now."

"Yes ma."

"You are clever." Mama Theresa smiled.

Chapter 2

Mama Theresa was the fourth wife of her husband and the favorite. This favoritism was not because she was the most beautiful or because she cooked better than all the other wives. She was the favorite because she was strong and enterprising. The other wives before her were not as clever and as prosperous as she was. While they went to the farm, Mama Theresa traded in town and because her husband was too old to farm, she took care of him. She was the favorite because it was said that she was the one who paid her own bride-wealth.

When the new religion came to Ugwuta, Mama Theresa together with Mgbada's mother embraced it. Both of them were christened Theresa. Mama Theresa suffered greatly. The preaching of the new religion was salutary. It gave her hope. She had buried all her children before they reached the age of five, and it was believed that her co-wives bewitched them.

Before the new religion came, she and her husband had been advised to go to the oracle in Arochukwu to find out the cause of her children's deaths. They set out and before they reached Arochukwu, they met some fellow travelers who advised them to return home, for great atrocities were perpetrated by the agents of the Oracle. So, they returned home.

A year later, Christianity came to Ugwuta. Mama Theresa embraced it. That same year, she gave birth to her daughter, Akpe, who was baptized as Maria. Her husband, unlike Mgbada's father, embraced the religion. He made his other wives join as well. But as time went on, the co-wives fell by the wayside. The demands of the new religion were too much. Even Mama Theresa's husband gradually went back to the worship of the ancestors before he died.

Mama Theresa stuck to the religion. Her daughter did not die when she reached the age of five. Her faith was responsible for this. She contributed a lot to the success of the church. She made sure that her husband's children went to school.

In the mornings, a big pot filled with yam was cooked while the children went to the Lake to have their bath and fetch water. Upon their return from the Lake, they dressed for school. When the yam was ready, the children ate it by first dipping it in a bowl of palm oil. Akpe particularly loved this meal. She did not care for the leftover cassava *foo-foo* and soup which the other children loved. So, sometimes while her brothers and sisters ate the cassava *foo-foo* she ate boiled yam and palm oil spiced with salt and pepper.

School was tough at the time. The teachers used the cane on the children at the slightest misdemeanor. In spite of this, Akpe liked school—unlike her sisters and a few of her brothers. One of her sisters refused to go to school after receiving six strokes of the cane from her teacher for coming late.

Back from school, they went to fetch firewood. Akpe and one of her sisters went to the market to help her mother sell and to bring back her wares each day.

In the evenings, after the meal, the storyteller told stories about the tortoise or the leopard and the dog. They also played hide and seek.

During the holidays, Akpe went with the other children to the farm. The children had so idolized the farm that she thought it was a land flowing with milk and honey, where fishes could be caught even by young children. She was disappointed. The children went by canoe and they had to paddle for hours before they finally came to the waterfront. Then they tied up the canoe and walked for more than three hours before they reached the farm settlement. By the time they arrived there, Akpe was so tired that she could not talk. One of her father's wives cooked a meal for them. She had thought that there would be plenty of fresh fish in the soup, but there was only miserable looking dried fish floating in the liquid that was called soup. Akpe did not complain. She ate quickly and wanted to go to bed. But she was told about the masquerade which would appear soon. So, she waited, for she was fond of masquerades. She soon fell asleep when the masquerade failed to appear. Then the mosquitoes took over. They sang in her ears. They bit her toes and fingers so much that she slapped and scratched all night. In the morning she cried and cried until one of the farmers took her home to her mother.

Akpe was fifteen years old when her father died. So, her mother withdrew her from school. Mama Theresa had hoped very much that she would send her daughter to a convent school where she would learn the art of keeping a Christian home. But the death of her husband changed all that. By the time the burial ceremonies were performed and the mourning period over, she was no longer in a position to send her daughter to Asaba Convent. But she did not despair. Time was passing. Education may even jeopardize her daughter's chances of getting a husband. It would be better if she had her children young.

It was obvious to Mama Theresa why her namesake was visiting her. There was no point in beating around the bush, so she asked, "Now tell me, Theresa, why have you paid me a visit?"

Silence.

Nwafor had rehearsed what she was going to say and how she was going to say it, but Mama Theresa's bluntness took her by surprise.

"You are very blunt."

"I am."

"I saw a pearl in your house."

"A pearl?"

"Yes, a jewel."

"Maria?"

"Yes, Maria."

"Go on."

"We want to marry her."

"We…?"

"My son."

"Joseph?"

"Yes, Joseph. I call him Mgbada."

"He is Joseph."

"Yes, he is Joseph. He is my son and he is interested in marrying your daughter. I hope you will agree that we marry your daughter."

Pause.

"Have you discussed this with your son?"

"My son and I speak in one voice."

"No, that's not what I mean. Is my daughter the choice of your son? That's what I mean."

"Yes, my son told me about your daughter."

"Good, you are not imposing your will on your son?"

"No," Nwafor said meekly, which was unlike her.

"All right, I have heard you. I am going to talk to my daughter when she returns."

"When shall I visit again?"

"Don't worry. I shall come to you."

"Don't make it too long. My son wants to marry immediately. We like you and we like your daughter."

"Don't say it again. You shall hear from me."

"Thank you, I must go now."

"Thank you for coming. Go well."

Some days later the mother of Akpe talked to Mgbada about the issue.

"I have talked to my daughter. She confirmed that she was interested in you."

"Yes, ma," replied Mgbada meekly.

"And you are interested in her?"

"Yes, ma."

"You are a Christian?"

"Yes, ma."

"Will you marry my daughter in the church?"

"Yes, ma."

"You will?"

"Yes, ma."

"But you have the *ofo* of your ancestors."

"That's right, ma."

"The God that we worship is a jealous God. You must not have any other God but Him."

"The God you are referring to is the God of the Hebrews," Mgbada thought. Why would he antagonize his would-be mother-in-law? He must be careful.

So, he said, "Yes, ma, I know."

"My son, I believe in the Almighty God and in His son. As far as I am concerned, you are either a Christian or you are not. Even those people who call themselves Christians and belong to the other church will not enter the Kingdom of God. The Roman Catholic Church is the one and only one. So, Father Millet taught us. Thank God that you belong to the Roman Catholic Church. If you had belonged to the other church, I would not have allowed my daughter to marry you, unless you were prepared to convert."

Silence.

"As a Christian," Mama Theresa went on, "You must respect the teachings of Christ. You must not associate with non-Christians. You must go to mass, go for confession, and receive the Holy Communion every Sunday."

"Yes, ma."

"Does 'yes, ma' mean that you agree with me?"

"I agree with you, ma."

"Good. And remember that as a teacher of the young in this town, you must show a good example. You should encourage the children of this town to embrace Christianity and also go to school. The white man has brought to our doorstep their religion and education. The world is changing. And those who do not follow the new teachings would be left behind."

"I agree, ma."

"I have a problem."

"Yes, ma?"

"I had wanted to send Maria to a convent, the one at Asaba, but her father died. Now she cannot go."

Silence.

"I wish I can send her."

"You mean before she gets married?"

"Yes."

"There is no need." His mother's words.

"No need?"

"Yes, no need. She will learn on the job." His mother's words again.

When Mama Theresa saw that she was not making any headway, she dropped the subject.

At the time Mama Theresa was preaching to Mgbada, Nwafor was probing Akpe:

"You like us?"

"Yes, ma."

"You would like to marry my son?"

"Yes, ma."

"Good. He is a good son. He is not a difficult person. He will do as you want him to do."

Akpe sat up. "Do as I want him to do?" she thought this over.

"You went to school?"

"Yes, ma." Akpe did not know where Nwafor was heading.

"You will want a church wedding?"

"Of…" she stopped. "Yes, ma."

"Mgbada will marry you in the church. I will see to that. But we have to perform the traditional rites."

"Yes, ma."

"Don't bother about going to Asaba convent."

Silence.

"Do you hear me?"

"Yes, ma."

"Marriage first before anything else. There is plenty of time for other things. Marry now and you will have your children when you are young."

"Yes, ma."

"Have you been circumcised?"

"No… yes, ma."

"Are you sure?"

"Yes, ma." Akpe was properly briefed before she saw Mgbada's mother.

"Are you sure that you have been circumcised?"

"Yes, ma."

"Because if you are not, you will not be able to have a child."

"Mother did not tell me so," Akpe said rather timidly.

"Don't bother about your mother and what she told or did not tell you."

Silence.

"Do you hear me?"

"Yes, ma. But she did not tell me that if I was not circumcised that I will not have a child."

"Forget about that."

"Yes, ma."

"So, you want us to come."

"Yes, ma."

"After the traditional marriage we shall perform the Christian one. Is that not what you agreed with your mother?"

"Yes, ma."

"We shall do as you say. My son is going to make you happy. He is a good son; you will grow to like him."

"Yes, mother."

But Nwafor knew that Akpe was not circumcised. So, she decided to see her namesake about it.

Chapter 3

"We must put our heads together, Theresa," Nwafor said.

"You mean the circumcision?"

"Yes, that's what I mean."

"You know it is dangerous?"

"I know."

"If you know, why must we think about it?"

"It is the custom of our people. If it is not performed, Akpe will not be able to have children."

"Theresa, you still believe that?"

"I do."

Silence.

"It depends on who does it," said Nwafor.

"Who do you have in mind?"

"Mgbeokworo."

"Mgbeokworo? I know her. Does she, do it?"

"Yes."

"But…"

"I have a plan. I know it is dangerous, and I have been told of young girls bleeding to death…"

"And you still want us to do it?"

"I told you I have a plan."

"Go ahead."

"We are two well-known women in this town, and…"

"Go ahead, I am listening."

"We must devise a means, a way out…"

"I am listening."

"Of making everybody believe that a circumcision had actually taken place."

They fell silent.

"I see, go ahead."

"We shall inform Mgbeokworo."

"She will come on the appointed day."

"To my house?"

"Yes, that's the custom."

"Go on."

"She will bring everything used in doing it, and everybody will know about it…"

"I understand. Then we bribe her and tell her not to do it."

"Exactly, and she would pretend that she had done it."

"That's all right by me."

"Good, only the two of us and Mgbeokworo will know what actually happened. Maria will not know."

"How will she not know?"

"Mgbeokworo will take care of that, and remember Maria told me that she was circumcised, so she doesn't really know what it is all about."

"I agree."

So, Akpe was 'circumcised'. The people were happy and satisfied that their tradition was not trampled upon by the new religion. Mgbada's mother gathered both the old and the young of the village for the traditional marriage. She also informed her own relations and the *umuada* that her son was going to take a wife. She bought all the palm wine, *kai kai* and Schnapps for the occasion. She bought kola nuts, salt and white chalk.

In the evening, she and her son together with the village people went to the house of Mama Theresa, who received them and took them to her daughter's uncle, who was the head of the family.

Akpe dressed casually. She was quiet and shy. Her face was blank. One was not sure whether she was happy or not. She looked mature and alert. She sat beside her uncle. Some of her friends sat beside her.

Kola nut was presented, it was broken and eaten. Likewise, palm wine and *kai kai* were also presented. Everybody present drank. The atmosphere was relaxed. The young men joked and made merry. Then Mgbada's people introduced the reason for their presence through their spokesman who said:

"We saw a gem in your family. Our son, who is also a gem, wants to make your gem his. Briefly, this is why we are here."

"Is this gem with you?" asked the spokesman from Akpe's family. "If he is here, can our daughter identify him?"

Akpe walked to Mgbada and took his hand. There was jubilation and a lot of noise.

"Our daughter, you have shown us your young man. He and his people are here. They have brought us drinks, and you know what that means. Now tell us, should we drink or should we not drink?"

There was silence.

"Go on, don't be shy, should we drink?"

"Drink," Akpe said shyly. There was another round of applause and jubilation.

"Isn't she smashing?" said one of Akpe's cousins.

"She is, she is, that's why our brother has gone all out for her," said one of Mgbada's cousins.

"I bet you don't have such daughters in your village," Akpe's cousin said.

"We do, my in-law, we do; keep your eyes open and you will see them—look, there's one over there. How does she compare with yours?" Mgbada's cousin asked.

"*Chaa sa*. No comparison, *ana eji akpu na agbayani ara?*" said Akpe's cousin.

"Look, man, mind what you say here; or..." That was Mgbada's cousin. "Look at this man from the farm; don't you have a sense of humor?"

"You call me a farmer, eh, you call me a farmer. You..."

"Hey, will you stop that? Why should you quarrel today of all days? Today we are giving our beautiful daughter away in marriage. Please, please. Here, have my drink... come closer, my in-law." There was laughter all around.

Akpe's uncle called everybody to order when the laughter subsided. "Now, listen, my people, listen, and don't make any more noise. Our in-laws are with us. We must be nice to them. Here are their kola nuts; we have not even broken them. The two young people have not been declared husband and wife yet. So, please keep quiet. He took one kola nut and began:

> *My people, here is kola nut*
> *Brought by our in-laws*
> *Our in-laws,*
> *To your health,*
> ***Ise.***
> *My people,*
> *To your health*
> ***Ise.***
> *It is the kola nut*

From the son of a great man
Ise.
It is the kola nut
For the daughter of a great man
Ise.
May our ancestors
Bless this kola nut
May our ancestors
Partake of this kola nut
Ise.
May our ancestors
Bless the union
Between our daughter
And our son
Ise.
May this union be fruitful
May these young people
Be blessed with offspring
Ise.
What we ask for them
We also ask for ourselves
Guard and protect us
Ise.

"Now come and share the kola nut."

Mgbada and Akpe knelt before the elder; Mgbada accepted the kola nut, bit a piece, and handed the other piece to Akpe whose uncle took the Schnapps and, pouring the libation, said:

> *Our ancestors*
> *Here is the drink*
> *Brought by our in-laws*
> *To your health*
> ***Ise**.*

He poured a generous amount on the floor, and the young men yelled jokingly in protest: "Father, what are you doing? Do you want our ancestors to get drunk? Don't give them too much to drink. They drank their share when they were with us."

"No," protested another: "Give them some to drink. They must be thirsty. Azaka, especially, must be dying to drink *kai kai*. I don't think they have *kai kai* over there."

Everybody laughed. The Schnapps was poured into a glass which was given to Mgbada by Akpe's uncle. He drank and gave some to Akpe to drink. This done, everybody began to drink and to make merry. At this time, more and more people arrived and were served.

Meanwhile, Mama Theresa and a few women chosen for the job began to cook. A goat had been slaughtered. The women busied themselves with washing the goat for soup and others were peeling the yams.

The elders of the two families had gone inside to

negotiate the bride wealth. When they finished, they needed to eat for the night was far gone and they were getting hungry.

Before the first cockcrow, the in-laws had eaten and were ready to take away their wife. Akpe was led to her new home by handpicked men from among her people. The procession trooped to the home of the eldest man of Mgbada's village. There Akpe was received; kola nut was eaten, more wine drunk and gifts presented.

A few weeks later, the church wedding took place. The mass was early. Akpe's uncle led her to the altar. She was a beautiful bride. She wore a white wedding gown made of soft lace and organdie, with silver sequins glittering on the neckline and the sleeves. Her veil was long. She had on a pair of white high-heeled shoes. Her chief bridesmaid wore a light blue chiffon gown. The six little bridesmaids wore yellow chiffon dresses.

Mama Theresa wore a long flowing white gown made of lace. She had on a wide-brimmed hat as was the fashion in those days. Nwafor wore velvet *up and down* and she adorned her neck with coral beads. She wondered why her namesake did not wear coral beads for this august occasion. "When would she wear them? Or has she sold them?" she thought.

Soon the church wedding was over, and a crowd of people accompanied by the school band marched the bride and the bridegroom to the school hall for the reception. The people danced to the band music and rice and flowers were sprinkled on the bride and the bridegroom. Mama Theresa danced and so did Nwafor. In the hall, the master of ceremonies spent a lot of time introducing the chairman of the occasion and the dignitaries. Guests were tired before the newly weds were ushered into the hall and to the high table. Madam Ogbuefi Ugo, Theresa's friend, was angry because she was not at the high table.

After prayers and the breaking of kola nuts, food and drinks were served. Some guests were not happy with what was going on. Those serving the foods and the drinks concentrated on the high table and some special areas of the hall. Madam Ogbuefi Ugo was now livid with anger. Why were they treating her like a poor relation? Didn't she attend this wedding to honor her friend's children and to donate generously? She called on one of the girls who was serving,

"Come, my daughter, do you think we have come here to play? Or to watch others eat and get drunk? Do you know me?"

"No, ma," the girl replied.

"You don't know me? You must be a stranger to this town. I am Ogbuefi Ugo. I am the friend of Theresa, the mother of the bride. I have not been served. Now go and get me something to eat and to drink. Do you hear?"

"Yes, ma."

"Go now or else I am going home with my donation. What sort of rubbish is this? Why should I be subjected to this humiliation? Why? Because I agreed to attend the wedding of my friend's daughter? And look at Theresa over there," she hissed.

She got up and marched to the high table, pointing at her friend. "Theresa, so you asked me to come here to be insulted? What do you think…?"

"Please, my good friend…"

Mama Theresa jumped up with the agility of a thirty-year-old woman.

"Please, my friend, please *ada ibe m*, not here. *Ewo-o*, who has done this? Come."

She grabbed Madam Ugo's hand, pleading:

"Sit here, yes, my seat, sit. Why should you stand while I am sitting? God forbid."

Madam Ogbuefi Ugo sat on Mama Theresa's seat while she went to bring something for her to eat and drink. Madam Ugo was triumphant:

"I have done it. Nonsense. Why should I be relegated to the background? Are all these people sitting here more important than me? Richer than me? Good. Didn't our people say that if you do not lick your lips then the *harmattan* will lick them for you?"

"Mama, you are right, you are right," said everybody at the high table.

"Thank you, my children. This place befits my status and stature. Don't you see how big I am? *Ehee ajigijim*."

Everybody roared with laughter.

"Now I can donate generously," she continued.

Mama Theresa brought her a plate of rice. A girl brought drinks. She began to eat.

Mama Theresa was not happy with how things were going. So, she went to where the food and drinks were kept and drove away all the unauthorized people:

"What do you think you are doing here, all of you? You have come here to eat? Who invited you? Go away, all of you, go away."

She came back to the bridal table and faced the chief bridesmaid and the bridesmaids. "Do you think that you are going to be served here? Nobody is going to serve you. Go and get your food, and don't be staring at the bridal table as if you have not seen food for the past ten days. Off you go."

But they stayed where they were.

"You can stay. Stay and die of hunger," she said, going to look for another seat.

"Mama, mama, he has put pepper in my eyes. My eyes, my eyes."

Mama Theresa turned.

"Who put pepper in your eyes?"

"I don't know. I don't know. My eyes-*oo*. They have blinded me-*oo*."

"You greedy children, who invited you? Eh, come here, try and open your eyes."

"I can't-*oo*. They have blinded me."

"Keep quiet and open them—let me blow into them."

"It was Adindu; he did it so that he can eat all the rice and meat."

The child was led out of the hall by one of the stewards, and the eating and the drinking continued.

The school brass band had started playing. Mgbada made sure that they had a good practice for the great day. But this was not the time to play music, his mother thought. She got up, went to her son and whispered in his ear:

"What are you doing? The band should not play now, the guests would be carried away; they will not remember to make their donations. How are we going to recover all the money we have spent on the wedding feast?"

"All right, mother," said Mgbada. He whispered to the master of ceremonies who promptly announced for donations. Many guests came to the bridal table and dropped their pennies and shillings. Some brought wrapped-up presents. When Madam Ugo got up, she donated one shilling and insisted that it must be announced. So, the master of ceremonies announced that Madam Ugo had donated twelve pennies!

Soon it was time to escort the bride and the bridegroom home. The chief bridesmaid was wiping

Akpe's face with a handkerchief. She was crying. It was expected of her to cry. She must not show that she was in a hurry to leave her father's house for her husband's place. As she prepared to leave the hall, her age-grade began to sing and to dance:

> *Onaa*
> *Ona be di ya*
> *Onaa*
> *Ona be di ya*
> *Echinine*
> *O'change a pillow*
> *She is going*
> *She is going*
> *To her husband's home*
> *She will change the pillow*
> *Tomorrow*
> *She will change the pillow.*

Akpe cried the more. Her age-grade was bidding her goodbye. She was one of them. Now her status had changed. She was now a married woman. She must now behave like one. The brass band played and slowly walked with the bride and the bridegroom as their well-wishers led them home. When they arrived home, the age-grade began to sing a new song, dancing and saying goodbye:

Maria
N'odu nma
Enwero n'chigha ozo
Maria
N'odu nma
Enwero n'chigha ozo
Eziokwu
Gwanu, Maria
Na nodu nma
Enwero n'chigha ozo
Maria, it is goodbye
There is no going back
Maria, it is goodbye
There is no going back
In truth, it is goodbye
Tell Maria
There is no going back.

Akpe began to cry openly as her age-grade sang and dispersed. Mgbada was embarrassed but he tried to wipe his wife's tears with his handkerchief.

Chapter 4

Ten months after the wedding, Mgbada and Akpe were blessed with a bouncing baby boy. Mgbada named him Aneneorisha. His age-grade and friends teased him while congratulating him.

"You must teach us your skill. How come you did not miss," said one.

"And not only that you did not miss, you had a boy," said another.

"Mgbada, you must let us in on your secret," said yet another.

"Are you seriously asking him to reveal his secret?" added another.

"Yes, why not?"

"I heard you," said Mgbada. "You know what you should do? "

"No," the man replied.

"You don't know what you should do?" asked Mgbada again.

"No, I don't know."

Silence.

"Tell us."

Silence.

"Why don't you want to tell us?"

Silence.

"Come on," everybody urged.

"Well, if you must know, send over your wives," said Mgbada.

The roof of the house nearly came down with the uproar that followed. Even the man that first asked the question laughed the loudest. Such was the sense of humor of the people.

The two mothers hurriedly began to put things together. They dared not do this before the arrival of the baby, for they would incur the wrath of the gods. So, palm kernel oil, soap, herbs, *wrappas*, towels were hurriedly put together. Akpe should have gone to the maternity home in the mission to have the baby, but he was two weeks early. A local midwife delivered the baby.

For twenty-eight days, Mama Theresa came to the house to give the newborn a bath. The bath was ritual in nature. The water used was boiled with herbs and some roots prescribed both by the midwife and Mgbada. The baby was scrubbed well with a special sponge and soap. Then the little boy was carefully dried with a towel, and palm kernel oil with herbs rubbed all over the tiny body.

The tiny hands and feet, including the toes and fingers, were stretched and massaged. The hair combed. Then the baby was wrapped up and handed over to his mother.

Also, for twenty-eight days, Akpe was pampered. Her mother made her sit in a basin filled with hot water and herbs. This was done for complete purification after childbirth. Special meals like pepper soup with dry fish, spices and herbs were prepared for her to help with digestion and strength building. Akpe enjoyed the attention. Her friends, age-grade and some *umuada* cooked for her and made things easy for her. Soon the twenty-eight days were over and she went to the Lake, put her feet in the water, and returned home. Then on Sunday she went to mass and her son was baptized. His name was Anthony, but everybody called him Orisha, the short form of Aneneorisha. Akpe was sewing one afternoon when her mother walked in.

"It is hot," she said.

"It is going to rain," Akpe said.

"You think so?" she looked at the sky.

"No, it is not going to rain. Look at the movement of the clouds. If it is going to rain the clouds would be here," she said, indicating where she meant with her forefinger.

"That's a beautiful dress you are making," she said to her daughter.

"Who are you making it for?"

"My mother-in-law."

"Your husband's mother?"

"Yes."

"Aren't you making one for your mother?"

"I will," Akpe said, sewing furiously.

"What is the matter with you?"

"Nothing."

"If there is nothing, then pay attention to me. Did you see me here yesterday?"

"Mother, what's all this?"

"What's all what? I came to see my only child and she behaves as if I am a creditor."

Akpe did not reply, she went on sewing.

"Are you well?"

Silence.

"Tell me are you well?"

"I am well."

"What then is the matter?"

Silence.

"Your husband?"

Akpe nodded.

"It has to come."

"What has to come?" Akpe asked.

"Husband and wife troubles."

Silence.

"You should not worry yourself. You don't have a co-wife."

Silence.

"You married in church. I made sure that you married in church. So, your husband will not marry another one. And besides, you have had a boy for him."

"It is none of that, mother."

"Then what is it? Why don't you take your mother into confidence? Did your husband beat you?"

"No," Akpe said, and wondered whether beating was an accepted practice in marriage.

"If you don't want to talk, I am going."

She re-tied her head-tie, adjusted her *wrappa* and was about to leave when her namesake returned.

"*Haa* my namesake, are you leaving? Sit down, let me find you something to drink—it is hot. Please sit down."

Mama Theresa reluctantly sat down while Nwafor put down her basket and went in search of kola nuts and ground nuts. She called from within, "Mother, can I bring you some dry fish, too?"

"All right, my daughter."

Nwafor laughed.

"Why are you laughing?" asked Mama Theresa.

"The way you address me."

"What is wrong with that? You called me mother, and I called you my daughter…"

"Yes, but…"

"We have gone into that several times. Just call me Theresa or namesake. Cut out the mother."

"But you are my mother. My son is married to your daughter. So, both my son and I are bound by tradition to call you mother."

"Agreed, but I said don't call me mother."

"It is a sign of respect."

"I know. It is unchristian."

"Unchristian? My namesake, the way you go about your religion is rather strange. All right, I have heard you. Here is kola, break it, let's eat. But didn't my son's wife give you kola?"

"She did not."

"My son's wife, why didn't you give your mother kola? Did you forget?"

She turned to Mama Theresa.

"My namesake, don't worry, she forgot, here is kola. I did not see you in the market yesterday. What happened?"

"My back, what else but my back."

"Did you see the doctor when he came last month?"

"I did. He gave me some medicines. I asked him to give me an injection but he refused."

"So, you are still having the pain?"

"Yes, then I asked Ojoru to draw out some blood from the place it was hurting most and…"

"When did you see Ojoru?"

"Last week. I had a little relief, but now the pain is back."

"Let my son look at you."

"Joseph?"

"Yes, let him look at you. He can help."

"Yes, I heard that many people come to see him these days after he cured a little girl of measles that killed nearly ten children in the village."

"That is true, but it was not measles, it was whooping cough."

"Whooping cough? That's even more fatal than measles. And he uses herbs, roots and water and some incantations to effect the cures. Is it true?"

"Yes, it is true. And he is now thinking of leaving teaching and concentrating on his skills as a medicine man," said Nwafor.

"No!" exclaimed Mama Theresa.

"Why do you say no?" asked Nwafor.

"Leaving teaching? Why should he abandon teaching for traditional medicine?"

"That's where his talent is, and I support him fully."

"Now I know why my daughter is unhappy," Mama Theresa thought. "Now I know that sooner than later he would fall, he would abandon Christianity."

"You don't seem to approve," said Nwafor.

"Who am I to approve or not to approve? Your son is a man. A man will do what he wants to do. No woman dictates to a man."

"You said so, not me."

"I know what I am saying. Don't believe those who say that I dictated to my late husband."

"I don't believe them. But I know that if it were not for you, he would not have been converted to Christianity."

"True, but he fell by the wayside when the going was rough."

"When they asked him to marry you in church and abandon his other wives?"

"Not only that; when his brother reaped the proceeds of the land belonging to their father without as much as informing him. My late husband called everybody, and the whole clan settled the misunderstanding. It was after that that he stopped taking the church seriously."

"Is that so?"

"He abandoned a seat in the kingdom of God for worldly gain. I am sorry for him."

Silence.

"And does my daughter know that your son wants to abandon teaching?"

"He must have told her."

"And does she like it?"

"She must. More money will come in. The people cured bring yams, fish, chickens and goats to my son. What wife would not like that?"

Silence.

"*Ahaa*, that's my son coming home," Nwafor said when she heard Mgbada's voice. "Welcome, my son."

"Welcome, my daughter's husband."

"Mother, it's good to see you. It is a long time. How is your back, much better?"

"It is still bad," Mama Theresa said.

"Ojoru drew blood from her back," added Nwafor.

"Ojoru again?"

"Why do you say that?"

"Because drawing blood is not good. You need all the blood in your body, you should not waste it. Please, mother, don't let Ojoru do it again."

"But I was relieved afterwards."

"It does not matter. Are you cured now?"

"No."

"That's what I mean. Can you come here tomorrow? I can cure your back for you."

"You can?"

"But I have told you several times that I can cure you. You don't believe me."

"All right, I shall come tomorrow. I believe you."

"Good, come before the sun is up. I have to get some roots which must be dug out and used before the sun comes out."

"I shall come."

"Where is my wife? Hasn't she heard my voice? Mother, isn't Akpe home? And Orisha, where is he?"

"Orisha and Uru have gone to play. I heard Akpe's voice a while ago." She called Akpe but there was no answer. "The kola nut, Joseph, break the kola for us. My namesake, where is the glass?"

Nwafor brought three small glasses; they ate the kola and drank the *kai kai*.

"Where did you say my wife went to?" asked Mgbada again.

Nobody replied.

"Mother," Mgbada turned to his mother-in-law. "Akpe is not happy with me."

"Why?"

"She thinks I am abandoning teaching."

"Are you?"

Silence.

"Are you?"

"Please mind how you talk to my son."

"I wasn't talking to you, Theresa."

"I didn't say you were talking to me."

"Please keep quiet, mother. My wife is not happy with me, I know. I have told her that I have a calling. I know a lot about medicines. I learnt a lot from my father who learnt from his father. I am a Christian. Even Christ cured the sick. I don't see why she should be upset. I am not leaving teaching tomorrow. I am merely thinking about it. So please tell her not to be upset. I shall continue to teach, go to mass, go to confession and receive the Holy Communion."

There was silence as these consoling words sank

in. Nwafor wasn't quite happy but said nothing. Mama Theresa was pleased. She, too, said nothing. At that moment Ojoru entered the house and greeted the women.

Ojoru ferried people across the Lake for a fee. On the side she drew blood from those who complained of pains. It was rather early for her to return home. She greeted Mgbada and the others, put her basket down, joined them. She was served kola nut and Nwafor gave her some *kai kai* to drink.

"Thank you, my sister. I am hungry; I want to eat first before I drink. Without food in my stomach, the *kai kai* will make me faint."

Nwafor got the message.

Ojoru continued, "Nwafor, my sister, I have food, but I don't have soup."

Mgbada smiled to himself.

"Teacher, are you laughing at me?"

"God forbid that I should laugh at you," denied Mgbada.

"I dare say. It is no crime to be poor. And why should I be shy to ask for soup from my sister Nwafor? Without my sister Nwafor, I would have been buried very many years ago. So, Nwafor…"

"Don't worry, Ojoru, you shall eat. There is no soup, but my son's wife will cook now. How did it go today on the Lake? You returned rather early."

The old woman shook her head sorrowfully before she began: "Why shouldn't I return home early? All the people I ferried across the Lake today paid me nothing."

"Why is that?" asked Mgbada.

"My brother, that's life. The people just refused to pay."

"But why do you ferry them if they don't pay?"

"My brother, how do I know that they have no money to pay? I don't collect money before they are ferried across. It is when I get to the other side that they pay. By the time I knew what was happening, they had jumped out of the canoe. The so-called good ones merely said, *"Mbona eemeka."* I asked them: "Will I eat *thank you*?" They laughed at me and went their way."

"That's terrible."

"Today was the worst day for me. So, I said to myself, I might as well go home and rest. Perhaps I have wronged the Woman of the Lake inadvertently. That's why I returned early."

"You did well," Mama Theresa said, and got up to go home. "Next time, the Woman of the Lake will break kola for you," she continued mockingly.

"*Ise*, may it happen as you say," Ojoru said.

"I named my only child after the Woman of the Lake. I named her Ogbuide because she was very beautiful. But she did not live. The Woman of the Lake took her from me."

"Took her from you?" asked Mama Theresa.

"Yes, she drowned after the flood when she was ten years old."

"So, it actually happened?" asked Nwafor.

"Didn't she know how to swim?" asked Mgbada.

"She could swim at the age of three. You know our custom. As soon as a child is able to walk, she learns to swim. That's why I said that the Woman of the Lake took her from me."

"To do what?" asked Mama Theresa.

"The Lake is mysterious," said Mgbada. "No one person can know the mysteries of the Lake. Our forefathers were fishing in Urashi River when they discovered the mysterious Lake. They were fascinated by its freshness, its depth, its color and its fishes. They came and settled down on its shores. And since that time, it has been mysterious. So, I do not doubt what Ojoru has said. Mother, didn't you hear of the war between us and those warlike people on the Urashi River? You know what happened to our enemies. Our forefathers evoked the spirit of the Lake to fight for them, and the Lake did. Our enemies' canoes sank on the Lake, all of them drowned."

"Is that why our people worship the Lake?" asked Mama Theresa.

"Exactly."

"It is wrong. We should worship only the true God."

"You are right. Some people think that the Lake is powerful and that it is owned by a woman, called Ogbuide. That's what some people believe."

"Do you believe?" asked Mama Theresa.

Silence.

"Do you?"

"Yes, I believe those who worship her. You know some rich women in this town believe that she makes them wealthy."

"When they worship her?" asked Mama Theresa.

"Yes, when they worship her," said Ojoru.

"And Ogbuide sometimes appeared to people in dreams."

"Has she ever appeared to you?" asked Mama Theresa.

"No," she replied. "I am old now. She appears to younger women."

"I see. I must get going. Thank you, Joseph. I will come for my back. My namesake, please find something for Ojoru to eat. Well... but where is my grandson? I have been here all this time and he is not yet back. Well, I am going home; let day break."

"Let day break," they all said.

"Mother, remember to come for your back," said Mgbada, coming out from his room.

"That's right. When?"

"At your convenience."

"Tomorrow then."

"Tomorrow. Let day break."

"Let day break, my son. Ojoru, let day break. My namesake, I am going; let day break."

"Let day break, mother."

Mgbada did not go to school. He stayed at home to prepare for the treatment of his mother-in-law. He must prove to her that he could cure her back. Of what use was he if he cured others but could not cure his wife's mother?

So as soon as the cock crew, he got up, went to the back of the house, eased himself and returned to the room. His wife was up, too, and was having her bath in preparation for the morning mass.

"I have to try my best to convince Akpe that the two religions can be practiced by one person, that one complements the other. I need a lot of patience, but I am going to continue trying." He cleared his throat and said, "Akpe, your mother will come this morning for her back."

"I know."

"Come back from your mass quickly so that you can help me treat her."

She was silent.

"Did you hear me?"

"I heard you. I shall come back quickly. I am not going to sleep in the mission."

"Good. I hear a new catechist has come to the parish."

"No, he has not come yet; we expect him next week. Would you like to visit him?"

"Of course. He will come to the school to see us, but I shall visit him. But you know how busy they are. Can you help?"

"The church committee can arrange that."

"All right, my wife."

Mgbada washed his hands and face, as he crouched on the floor of his hut. Then he evoked the spirits of his ancestors to be with him, to give him power to cure his mother-in-law of her ailment. This done, he waited for Mama Theresa to come. She came home with Akpe after the morning mass.

"Mother, welcome."

"My son-in-law, thank you. So, you have refused to go to mass. "

"I go when I am less busy."

"I see."

"Akpe, please bring kola nut for your mother."

"Leave out kola this morning."

"I have to break kola nut and pour libation for our ancestors, mother."

"Can't you leave the ancestors alone?"

"I can't. They guide us. They give us strength. Without them, we are nothing."

"Without God, we are nothing."

"Of course. God is far away. So, we ask our ancestors to intervene for us. They are mere messengers. We can reach them through sacrifices, through incantations."

"Sacrifices?"

"We have to sacrifice to them."

"But..."

"There is no clash. We can still worship our ancestors and be Christians. When our ancestors demand a goat, we give them a goat. When they demand a chicken, we give them. You see they are here with us. As I am talking to you, they are listening, milling around, protecting us from our enemies, and from sudden death. The only problem is that we cannot see them with our own eyes. I know that if I fast, if I keep myself holy, if I am pure, and I evoke them, I can see them with my own eyes."

"You know that little children can see our ancestors in the form of spirits. That is why they are called spirits, *umummo*. Sometimes you see a child playing in the sand, and she begins to address people you do not see; but she sees them. My sister, who is dead now, was fond of speaking to spirits. She would pretend, I should not say pretend because she was not pretending, she saw the people she was addressing. She would say while playing: "Now you," she would mention a name, "now you go home and show your mother what you have bought from me. You can see I have not cheated you. So don't come back and say I have cheated you." Then she would turn to another: "Go home. I have said I am not going with you. All right, you stay there and wait. You cannot drag me away. I said I don't want to go home with you, do you hear?"

"Now if we disturbed her, she would come back to our own world, looking blank, sometimes embarrassed. If you asked her whom she was talking to, she would stare back at you. So, you see what I mean. There is the Supreme God. There are lesser gods, there are the ancestors. They play their own part in their own realms."

"Tell me about your back. When did you start having the pain?"

"Many years ago."

"When exactly?"

"After the birth of Maria."

"That's really a long time ago. Can you tell me how it started?"

"I have forgotten. It is a long time."

"Touch where it is painful."

She touched her waist.

"It is not your back, but your waist."

"It is all one and the same."

"Yes, something was not in place after the birth of my wife. Was it a difficult birth?

"No."

"You don't like hot water?"

"No."

"What will cure you is hot water."

"Hot water?"

"Only hot water with some herbs in it."

"Go on."

"I shall pluck the herbs myself. My wife will boil them for you and make sure that you sit in a basin filled with the boiled herbs two times a day for seven days."

"Seven days?"

"Morning and night for seven days." She nodded. "After seven days, come and tell me how you feel."

"Is that all?"

"It is all for the time being."

"Nothing to drink?"

"No."

"Nothing to rub?"

"No. Come after seven days. I will take care of the rest of the cure."

"No sacrifice?"

"Why do you worry about that? If I am asked to sacrifice, I shall do so on your behalf."

"On my behalf?"

"Yes."

She thought this over, and said, "When does the treatment begin?"

"I shall pluck the herbs today at sunset. Akpe will bring them to your house after her morning mass. In your house, she will boil the herbs. Try and sit in the basin of hot water."

Seven days later, Mama Theresa's ailment was cured.

"I feel new," she told Mgbada's mother.

"I told you. You were underrating my son. You see? Did he ask you to make sacrifices?"

"No."

"You see?"

Mama Theresa nodded. "I can bend down and pick up the broom from the floor. My namesake, I can sweep the floor now. Hot water is medicine by itself."

"And the herbs."

"And the herbs, my namesake. I screamed like a child when my daughter pressed me down in the basin of hot water. After the initial burning and pain, it was soothing."

"Can you bathe with hot water now?"

"Not yet. But when I have pain in any part of my body, I boil water and apply it on the pain."

Mgbada's fame echoed throughout the length and breadth of the land. Ojoru was the first to come, and when she was cured, elderly women, those suffering from arthritis, flocked to Mgbada's house and he cured them all.

Chapter 5

Akpe was pregnant. She had two children after Aneneorisha. It was a difficult pregnancy and her mother and Mgbada's mother were worried. But Mgbada assured them that there was no cause for alarm.

He made the necessary sacrifices, but he was not happy with the signals he was receiving from the spirit world. The diviners he consulted gave him conflicting messages: sacrifice to the earth goddess, sacrifice to the Lake goddess; sacrifice to the goddess of the road. The goddess of the road, that was new.

"Why must I sacrifice to the goddess of the road?" he asked.

"To clear the road for the easy passage of the unborn child," said a diviner.

Mgbada was silent.

"What kind of child will it be?"

"A strange child."

"Abnormal?"

"No, strange."

"Strange? I do not understand."

"A bouncing baby girl."

"She will not be the first."

"I know. You already have Idenu, but…"

"But what?"

"You have to take care of her."

"Idenu?"

"Yes, so that she can stay."

"She does not want to stay with us?"

"I have not said so."

"You have said so. If she does not want to stay, let her go now, now that we have not counted her."

"Don't be harsh."

"I am not harsh. The child who does not want to stay with its parents must go back to the spirit world."

"You are harsh."

"Perhaps. My mother suffered."

"Your sister?"

"My sister. She was that kind of child. She nearly killed my mother. Let me tell you what happened before she died. One night she was very ill. My mother was ill, too, but she ignored her own illness. She put her on her back, tied her securely, took the paddle, went down to the lakefront, took a canoe and paddled to the other side. She went to the *dibia* who lived at Ngo."

"I know him."

"The Igara *dibia*."

"A very good children's *dibia*."

"So mother said. There was no one with her. I was very small then. Father was drunk and was of no use. Mother prayed as she paddled the canoe. She saw no one, no human, no spirit, no ghost, just the expanse of the Lake. When she got to Ngo, she walked to the *dibia's* house. She woke him up. Good man, he was up as soon as he heard mother's voice. Mother untied the child. She was already dead."

"So, it really happened?"

"Mother wept like a human being; she wept like a beast in the forest. The *dibia* consoled her. He wanted her to stay and go home in the morning, but she refused. In her anguish she defied fear, put her dead child on her back, walked to the lakefront, stepped into the canoe and paddled home. By the time she got to the middle of the Lake, there was lightning and thunder. It began to rain. My mother paddled on. She could not see, but she went on paddling home. All was quiet, only the sound she made with the paddle and the sound of the thunder were heard. Her clothes were drenched by the rain, the dead child was drenched."

"Father's head cleared; he was no longer drunk when she returned. Calmly she put her dead child down."

"She is dead?" asked father.

"Yes. Find the men to dig the grave," said mother.

"Wait for cockcrow."

"No. Find the men now or I shall dig the grave and bury her myself," said mother.

"Before mother buried my sister, she drew a line on her forehead saying, 'If you come again, I am going to kill you.' You'll see."

"Your unborn child is not this kind of child."

"Are you sure?"

"I am sure."

"She is not abnormal?"

"No."

"Tell me now, for if she is abnormal, we shall prevent her from being born. There is no abnormality in our family."

"Young man, take your time," the *dibia* warned. He went on, "You came to me. I know you are a diviner like me. I know your father and your grandfather. Your child will be a strange child. That has been revealed to me. You cannot see it. A *dibia* does not cure himself. What is revealed to me about your unborn child cannot be revealed to you, because you are bound to your child by blood."

"I understand."

"Good. Take good care of your wife and sacrifice to the road. The journey from the spirit world to our world is long and trying. Sometimes the unborn children get tired on the way and prefer not to go further. Your child should have been the first one. She was not sure whether she wanted to be born to you or not. She kept waiting, going forward and backward. This time, she can no longer go back. She has a purpose in this world. She cannot postpone her coming any longer. Make it easy for her."

"I shall, our gods and ancestors being with me."

"Good, handle your wife kindly."

"I am not unkind to her."

"You speak like an ordinary man. You know what I mean."

"I know."

"So, why do you protest?"

Mgbada was silent.

"You came to me. I know what I am talking about. We live in interesting times. We see and don't see a lot of things. But those who have sharp eyes, eagle eyes, piercing and penetrating eyes, could see far. Our ancestors are all over the place, why do we feed them? Why do we give them food to eat and wine to drink? You see."

Mgbada nodded.

"Go home, perform the sacrifices. Take care of your wife. And…" he hesitated, "and don't touch her."

"Eh?"

"Yes. Don't touch her again."

"I understand."

"You should understand. Your father's father was a medicine man. Your father also. As for you, you have watered down your own powers with the new religion. But don't worry. You are still on the right path. Our ancestors protect you and your family."

He broke the kola nut. They ate; *kai kai* was brought and they drank. Mgbada went back home.

Mgbada took over the medical care of his wife. He did exactly as he was told. He prepared herbs, roots and all kinds of concoctions for his wife to drink. Akpe protested, but the two mothers prevailed on her to do exactly as she was told. The pregnancy reached the ninth month and nothing happened. Mgbada went back to the medicine man.

"I warned you," he began. "You must persuade her to be born. Not all of them want to come to our world. They are much better off in their own world, where there is no hunger, no suffering, no heat, no cold; where everything is serene and in the right proportions; where there is no pain, but joy and happiness."

"What must I do?"

"Continue to sacrifice, to woo her to come to the world, to be born to your wife, to be your second daughter. She will be born, of course. It has been written that she will be your second daughter. But in case of accidents, or the evil machinations of witches and wizards, especially witches—they are more diabolical—you must double your efforts at sacrifices. I forgot to give you something for the unborn child. I have prepared it, and here it is."

He gave him a very smooth, white round stone.

"Keep it until she is born. Then, when the umbilical cord falls, take it, wrap it around the stone. Tie it tightly with a piece of white thread. Leave it in your wife's *uko*. Twenty-eight days after the birth of your child, take it down and keep it in a safe place. Don't lose it! And don't let your child see it. Go well. And may our ancestors protect you and your family."

A week into the eleventh month, Akpe was in labor. The local midwife was called in and before any of the mothers arrived, Akpe gave birth to a bouncing baby girl. Nwafor came in. The baby yelled, and kicked its tiny legs. She seemed displeased with everything around her. Still kicking and yelling, she put three fingers into her mouth and sucked greedily.

Nwafor said, "Why are you protesting so much? Who kept you in your mother's womb all these months, eh? Who kept you? Answer me, my son's daughter. Didn't you want to be born? You are born and there is nothing you can do. Or do you want to go back to the spirit world? Do you miss your spirit companions? You are our daughter. We are going to take care of you. So, stop yelling. I want to clean you up nicely. That's my daughter. *Ewoo*, such long legs, hands and feet! Look at her fingers, so long, so well-formed. You are beautiful, my daughter. We shall take care of you. Do you hear?"

"Tell me, my daughter, why did you live so long in your mother's womb?"

The newly born baby yelled in protest.

"Oh, I should not ask you? You are something else, this child. You are sucking again. You want to eat. You are hungry? Look, look at her eyes. Those are not the eyes of a baby born moments ago. What, you are an old woman. Are you my grandmother?"

She kicked furiously.

"No, no, that's all right. I was merely joking. You are not my grandmother. My son, you have another daughter. Come, everybody, my daughter-in-law has given birth to a bouncing baby girl. The child that nearly killed its mother is born. The child that nearly sent her mother to the land of the dead is only a girl. A mere girl with a vagina and a womb. God, I thank you. Jesus."

The local midwife snatched the baby from Nwafor and proceeded to clean her up. Then Mgbada came to the room. He watched as the midwife cleaned the baby.

"Is my wife all right?"

"She is all right" the local midwife assured him.

He went over to Akpe. She was tired, but all right.

"May God be praised," Mgbada said.

When the local midwife finished cleaning the baby, Mgbada took her, sat down on a small low stool, placed the baby on his lap and proceeded to examine her closely. This done, he began:

Welcome, my daughter
You are my second daughter
I don't know why you chose me
As your father
Or why you chose my wife
As your mother
All I know is this:
You are going to be great
I don't even know
What your mission
On this earth will be
I cannot see it yet
But I know you are
Going to be a special person
Welcome, my daughter.

I can see the feather
On your forehead
Yes, a feather
Given to you by
The Supreme God
Through our ancestors
I welcome you my daughter
I can see your eyes

These are not the eyes
Of a baby born a few
Minutes ago
These are the eyes
Of an adult
Of a full-grown woman
Why do you open them so wide?
To see more?
You have already seen too much
Before you were born
Welcome, my daughter.

Your mother and I
Will take good care of you
In the best way we can
Since you chose us
As your earth parents
We shall bring you up
Just as our own parents
Brought us up
I am going to teach you
The ways of our ancestors,
Our traditions and customs
Your mother will teach you
The new religion
She knows it more than I do
More than I care to know

Though I am a teacher
Welcome, my daughter.

I am going to call you
Ona
You are a precious one
Ona, welcome
The whole world greets you
On your birthday
Welcome, my daughter.

Mgbada put down his daughter, and without speaking to anyone, he went to the back of the house. He picked some leaves. He dug up some roots and returned to his hut. He spoke to no one. The neighbors had filled the hut and were congratulating the mother of the baby. There was so much noise. He made signs which meant that everyone should leave. The local midwife asked everyone to leave. They left one after the other thanking God, the goddesses and ancestors for the new baby.

Mgbada shut the door, and opened the tiny window to let in the sunshine. The baby had been given some water to drink while she waited for the mother's milk to begin to flow. She was quiet now. Mgbada's mother was busy preparing pepper soup made with *uziza* for Akpe. Mgbada took the baby again. He repeated some incantations. He put the baby down. He crushed the leaves in the palm of his hands, and dropped a little water into it. Then he rubbed his palm on the body of the baby, talking to himself in a low tone. Then he handed over the baby to his mother and went out of the hut. In his hut, he invited some neighbors who were still milling around to drink with him. Glasses were brought. Palm wine and *kai kai* were served and they drank and made merry.

Chapter 6

Ona was like any other normal child. She was beautiful. Mgbada kept to himself what the diviner and medicine man had told him. He watched his daughter grow and was delighted with her. He took her to the Lake and bathed her. He discovered that she loved water and that she was quick to learn how to swim. In fact, before she was two years old, she had learnt how to swim and could swim out into the deep water. Her brothers and sister called her a fish because she swam better than they did.

So, one day when Ona was nearly three years old, her mother took her to the Lake to wash clothes and fetch water. While Akpe washed her clothes, Ona swam. She had an eye on her all the time, for her husband had warned her never to leave her unattended in the Lake.

"Mother I am swimming."

"I know you are swimming."

"I like the water."

"Yes."

"It is sweet."

"Go on and swim, but don't go far."

"Why?"

"The Woman of the Lake."

"Does she take small children?"

"No."

"Does she take big people?"

"No."

"Where is she?"

"She lives at the bottom of the Lake."

"All by herself?"

"Yes, all by herself."

"She has no mother?"

"No."

"No father?"

"No."

Ona was silent.

"No mother, no father. She dropped from the sky?"

"Perhaps."

"How old is she?"

"Many many years old."

"Uncountable years old?"

"Yes, uncountable."

"Is she from Ugwuta?"

Akpe pondered the question. Then she said, "Go on and swim."

Ona went to swim. She quickly returned and said, "What is her name?"

"We call her Ogbuide."

"Ogbuide?"

"Yes."

"What other name do you call her?"

"Uhamiri."

"Uhamiri," she repeated.

"Yes."

"And she has no father and no mother. Does she cook under the water?"

"She is a spirit."

"Does she not eat?"

"Spirits don't eat."

"I want to be a spirit."

"You cannot be a spirit."

"Why not?"

"You are a little girl. You are my daughter. You cannot be a spirit."

"Who lives with Ogbuide?"

"Nobody. She lives alone."

"I want to live with her."

"Are you sure?"

"Yes."

"But you cannot live with her."

"Don't little girls live with Ogbuide?"

"No."

"Can you live with her?"

"No."

"Why?"

"She is a spirit."

"Have you seen her?"

"No."

"Why?"

"Go on and swim. You are asking too many questions."

"If I dive into the water, will I see her?"

"I said, go and swim. Here, rinse this dress for me."

"It is Idenu's dress."

"Yes, it is."

"I won't rinse it."

"Why?"

Ona was silent.

"Tell me why."

"She calls me a fish."

"She calls you a fish?"

"Yes."

"Why does she call you a fish?"

"I don't know."

"Ask her when she returns from school."

"No."

"Why?"

"She will beat me."

"She won't. I am going to see to it. She won't beat you. She is your sister."

"She is not my sister."

"Idenu?"

"Yes."

"Idenu is my daughter. You are my daughter too. So, you are sisters."

"I have no sister."

"All right, go and swim."

Ona threw away Idenu's dress and jumped into the water and swam out of sight like a fish.

"What kind of child is this?" Akpe said as she rinsed her clothes. "I don't have to worry. She will not drown, that I know," she said and went on washing her clothes.

When she finished, she shouted Ona's name: "Come, let's go home now. You have swum enough."

"I am coming," Ona answered.

Ojoru, the ferrywoman, came to the lakefront. Akpe greeted her. "Is that Ona?"

"Yes."

"Ona, my daughter, you have grown. But you must be careful. Akpe, please don't let her swim so far out. The Lake is mysterious. Ona, do you hear?"

Ona nodded.

"Good girl. Akpe, please dry her body. She is cold."

Akpe dried Ona's body and rubbed palm kernel oil. She dressed her up, combed her hair, and they walked home. Ona was lagging behind.

"Is the pot too heavy for you?"

When she was close enough to be heard she said that it was heavy but that she could manage.

"No, you cannot manage. The pot of water is too heavy; I can see your neck. Put it down. Let me help you."

Ona stretched her neck and wiped the sweat from her face with the palm of her hand.

"We still have a long way to go; so, rest before we start again."

"I have rested."

"Rest, my daughter. When you are old enough, you will go to school with your brothers and Idenu."

"I don't want to go to school."

"Why?"

"I don't want to go."

"Your father went to school, I too went to school."

"I want to be a fisherwoman."

"A fisherwoman?" Akpe was silent, and she said, "That is all right. A fisherwoman can go to school. After going to school you can go and fish with small children like you in the village."

"Is that so?"

"Yes, it is so."

"Today is Nkwo."

"Yes."

Ona was silent.

"Today is Nkwo. Are you a market woman?"

"No."

"Why do you ask then?"

"Nothing."

"Mother, home is so far away today."

"We shall soon get home, don't worry."

"And there is nobody coming to the Lake, why?"

"Because today is Nkwo. Market women have gone to the market. This is not the way they take on market days."

"I know, this is the path taken by Ogbuide. Perhaps she will go to the market today."

"How do you know?"

"Grandmother told me. And last Nkwo when I went to the Lake with grandmother, I saw Ogbuide. She was returning from the market. She was dressed in velvet and coral beads. Her hair was very long. She could sit on it. Mother, I saw her."

"You are full of imaginations, my daughter."

"Mother, believe me, I saw her. And she greeted me."

"Did your grandmother see her too?"

Ona thought before she answered:

"She did not tell me."

"And you did not tell her that you saw Ogbuide?"

"No, I did not tell her."

"So, you have no witness?"

"Witness? What is a witness?"

"Somebody who saw Ogbuide with you."

"No. I don't need a witness."

"Come, let's go home now."

"Mother, I am serious. The day I saw her, she took me to her dwelling place."

"Really?"

"Yes, mother."

"You dream a lot, Ona."

"Mother, it was not a dream. She told me to come with her. So, I went with her."

"Is that so?"

"Yes, mother."

A snake crossed the road.

"Oh my God protect us."

"Mother, it is not harmful."

"How do you know?"

"I saw this kind of snake at Ogbuide's place."

"You did?"

"Yes. There were many of them. And Ogbuide talked to them."

"Is that so?"

"And also, there were other animals. I don't know their names. Ogbuide talked to all of them, and they laughed and clapped their hands."

"And clapped their hands? Snakes don't have hands and feet."

"The ones I saw at Ogbuide's place have hands and feet. Some have wings even."

"Wings to fly?"

"I don't know."

"Did you not see fishes there as well?"

"Plenty of fishes. Some were as big as our house. Some as tiny as Idenu's finger."

"Why Idenu's finger?"

Ona was silent.

"Tell me, why Idenu's finger? You don't seem to like her."

"I don't like her."

"Why?"

"She does not want to stay."

Akpe's basin of clothes nearly fell off her head.

"This child, this Ona, is strange. God please protect us. Ona, why do you say that?"

"Idenu will leave us one day."

Akpe said nothing.

When they got home, Akpe told her husband what Ona said. Mgbada in turn narrated to her an incident that occurred when Ona was only one and a half years old:

"One day after the evening meal, I was sitting outside the house drinking *kai kai*. You must have gone to see your mother. Ona came and sat at my feet. Soon she fell asleep. When I took her to her mat in your room, she woke up and began to cry. She said she did not want to go to bed.

"So, I took her back to my chair. She soon fell asleep again. Her brothers and sister teased her and I scolded them. Then, Ona opened her eyes wide, got up, and took my hand. I followed her. We went to the back of the house. She said to me: "You see the shrub over there. When they come tomorrow with the sick child, pluck the tender leaves from the shrub, wash them thoroughly. Put them in the small mortar. Then pound them, drop some water into the mortar and pound again. Put it in a cup. Add more water. Drain it and keep it for a while. After speaking to the parents of the child, give the juice to the child to drink. The parents of the child will come to you the following day to report that their child is well again. Then ask them to sacrifice to the Goddess of the Water. Then you…"

"She said no more. It happened as she said. I did not want to upset you by telling you; so, I kept it to myself. Now that you have noticed, we have to put our heads together and help our daughter so that she would live and fulfil the purpose for which she came to the world."

"What purpose?"

"It has not been revealed to me yet, nor to any of the diviners that I have seen."

"What about Idenu?"

"What about her?"

"Ona said that she would not stay with us."

"She said so?"

"She did. I have noticed, she does not like her sister."

"We have to be vigilant."

It was not long after this that the family woke up and found that Ona was not sleeping with her sister. Akpe raised an alarm. Mgbada tried to calm her down but to no avail. They looked everywhere; she was nowhere. Neighbors gathered and a search party was organized. Then it occurred to Mgbada to look where the sheep and goats were kept. He opened the crude door; the goats and sheep rushed out. Then he saw a pair of eyes staring from the darkness.

"Ona," Mgbada called.

"Mm."

"Ona."

"Mm."

"Come out."

She came out.

"Who took you there?"

"I don't know."

"Someone must have taken you there."

She stared back at her father.

"What were you doing among the sheep and goats?"

"Nothing."

"Nothing?"

"Nothing."

"How did you open the door?"

"The door was open."

"Our own door?"

"Yes."

"No, I locked the door myself. I was the last to go to bed. When did you leave the sleeping mat?"

"I don't know."

"You know nothing."

"Nothing."

"She will tell you nothing," said Akpe.

"Leave her to me. Ona, tell me, tell your father. He will understand," said Mgbada.

"She took me there."

"She did?" Akpe said, fear in her voice.

"She took you there?"

"Yes."

"Who is she?"

"She said I should follow her. So, I followed her. She walked fast. I could not keep up the pace, so I hid. She will come again."

"Would you like to follow her?"

Ona said nothing.

"Tell me."

She began to cry.

"Why are you crying?"

"She walked very fast. She left me behind."

"So, you would have followed her?"

Ona said nothing, and continued to cry.

"Why are you crying?"

"I am hungry. And I smell of urine. I am ashamed. I never wet the mat."

"Don't worry, we shall clean you up."

"Idenu will laugh at me."

"She has gone to school, don't worry."

"I am hungry and I want to sleep."

"Eat first."

Ona nodded. Akpe prepared food; Ona ate and went to sleep. The following day Akpe announced that she would send Ona to Father Millet.

"What will the Irish Priest do for Ona?" the bewildered husband asked.

"He will help her to be normal. She is possessed by the devil. Father can drive away the devil. You remember how Christ drove away the devil out of a man…"

"'And the devil went out of the man and entered into a herd of swine…" Akpe, I know my New Testament. The devil if I may say so, which possesses our daughter is a devil indigenous to our culture. The one in the New Testament is a Jewish one."

"Father will help us."

"I am a medicine man. I can help our daughter. Father Millet cannot help us. The spirit of the water possesses Ona; I think we can help her and ourselves by sacrifices to the Goddess of the Lake or to the earth goddess or both."

Akpe was not interested in what her husband said.

With the help of her mother, they sent Ona to Father Millet. As a result, Mgbada resigned from teaching, took up fishing on a larger scale, divined, cured and prescribed sacrifices for his clientele. Mama Theresa was confused. She had doubts about her faith. She prayed asking for strength.

Chapter 7

Ona was about twelve years old when she went to the convent in Ugwuta. There were about fifteen students; Ona was among the youngest. The convent was run by a widow who was a religious fanatic. She was called Madam Margaret. She was mean, hard and evil. She made the girls do all sorts of menial jobs including fetching water and collecting firewood.

Ona hated the convent from the first day her mother took her there. Her problem was compounded when Madam Margaret learnt from her mother why she was there: "You child of the devil" was how she addressed Ona from the day she arrived at the convent. "If you do not repent, you are going to hell." Then she painted a picture of hellfire as if she had seen it and said:

"The fire cannot be quenched. It burns all day and all night. When it burns you, you do not die. You continue to burn again and again. You do not die, because you had already died. Do you hear me? This is the way all those who do not belong to the church will burn in the never quenching fire."

"Madam," one of the older girls asked, "What about those who go to the other church, will they also burn in the hellfire?"

"All of them. Didn't you hear what Father Millet said? All of them will burn. Our church is the only true church. We say in the creed, 'I believe in the Holy Ghost, the Holy Catholic Church…'"

"You heard, the Holy Catholic Church," confirmed one of the girls who was becoming a fanatic.

The older girl said, "It is a pity. I know many of them who are good."

"Whether you are good or bad is not important. What is important is the church you attend. The true church is our own."

All this did not make any sense to Ona. Madam Margaret continued:

"And that is why you must not step into the premises of the other church. You remember how our Father punished the girls who were seen there during their harvest?"

The girls confirmed that they were witnesses to the severe punishment.

"Is Caro here?" Caro stood up. "You all should emulate her," Madam Margaret continued.

"A rich man came to ask her hand in marriage. The greedy parents who were pagans readily agreed without finding out the church to which the man belonged. It turned out that this man was a staunch member of the other church. Can you imagine that? Caro, good girl, refused to marry the man unless he converted to the true church. The greedy parents drove her out of their home and Caro ran to us. Here she is. Rather than gain worldly riches, she chose to come to this convent, to worship and serve her own God, and be saved from hellfire. Caro, sit down, my child. You are a good child. God will reward you."

"And we have children here possessed of devils. These children are children of the devil. How can a child born of Christian parents, a child whose parents were married in the church, a child who was baptized, be the child of the devil? Ona, will you get up?" Ona got up and bowed her head. "Look at her. She does nothing but swim in the Lake. She is afraid of school, so her mother told me. Father Millet will cure her; he will lay his hands on her head and cure her. Because she likes to go to the water, she must not be allowed to go near water, be it the stream, the river or the Lake. Report her, any of you, if you see her going to fetch water or swim. Our people lie to us by telling us that a woman lives at the bottom of the Lake. Do you agree?"

"No."

"Do you believe?"

"No."

"Good, how can a human being, a woman for that matter, live at the bottom of the Lake? Only fishes live in water."

"She is not a woman, she is a spirit. We do not see spirits but they are with us. The Woman of the Lake is with us all the time; just as God is with us all the time. So..."

"Ona, what has possessed you?" Madam Margaret asked in terror.

"Ogbuide."

"Wait here, Ona." Madam Margaret said and dismissed the other girls. "Have you seen her?"

"Who?"

"The Woman of the Lake."

"No, I have not seen her."

"And you say she is not a woman."

Silence.

"Can't you talk?"

Silence.

Madam Margaret decided to report Ona to Father Millet who was not making any headway in curing Ona. Father Millet called in the catechist who was a native and a fanatic like Madam Margaret. The catechist served as the interpreter. Ona was ushered into the presence of Father Millet. She was asked to sit down. She was afraid of Father Millet. His height, his long white beard and his priestly robes frightened her. She was asked to relax and to answer the Father directly. Then the Father prayed and the interrogation began:

"You love water."

"Yes."

"Why do you love water?"

Silence.

"Why? Tell us."

"I drink water."

"Everybody drinks water."

"Yes."

"Why do you love water?"

"Ogbuide is there."

"Ogbuide? Who is Ogbuide?"

Silence.

"Who is Ogbuide?"

"She is a spirit."

"Spirit?"

"Yes."

"Good or bad spirit?"

"Good spirit."

"And she lives in the water?"

"She lives in the water."

"She is a woman?"

"She is a woman."

"So, she cannot be a spirit."

Silence.

"Do you know her?"

Silence.

"Talk, do you know her?"

Silence.

"Does she talk to you?"

"Yes," Ona replied with no hesitation.

"What does she say to you?"

Silence.

"She says nothing to you?"

Silence. Ona began to bite her finger.

"Don't bite your finger."

She quickly removed her finger from her mouth. Father Millet and the catechist conferred with each other and afterwards continued the interrogation.

"You know why your mother brought you here?"

"No," Ona replied without hesitation again.

"You don't know?"

Silence.

"Your mother brought you here so that we can pray for you. An evil spirit is troubling you. So you are here in order that we can help you and make you a good Christian girl."

Silence.

"So, we want you to help us to help you."

Silence.

"So, what does this Ogbuide say to you?"

Silence.

"Does she tell you to harm people?"

"No."

"Does she tell you to beat up people? Does she give you things?"

"Yes."

"Like?"

"Fish. She sometimes shows me herbs."

"Herbs?"

"Yes, to cure the sick."

"You have used the herbs?"

"My father uses the herbs."

"Do you want to stay here with us?"

"No."

"We shall pray for you so that you will be a normal girl."

"There is nothing wrong with me."

"But you sometimes disappear."

Silence.

"And that was why your mother sent you to us. Why do you disappear?"

Silence.

"You don't know why?"

"I don't know."

"You just disappear?"

"Yes."

"What can we do for you?"

"Send me back home."

"You don't like the mission?"

Silence.

"You want to go home?"

"Yes, to my father."

"To your father, not your mother?"

"To my father and mother."

Father Millet and the catechist talked in whispers. Then the Father asked Ona to kneel down so that he could pray for her. She and the catechist knelt down, and after the prayer, she was taken back to Madam Margaret who was instructed to watch her closely. Madam Margaret knew that the Father had not made any progress. So, she continued to harass Ona.

"So, you are back."

Silence.

"Child of the devil."

Silence.

"On that day, when the righteous would be raised from the dead, the angels would descend from heaven and we the righteous would be taken up into heaven. There we shall be with the God Almighty and with Jesus Christ. And… do you doubt me?"

Silence.

"Child of the devil, get a bucket of water and a rag. I want us to clean the statue of our Mother and her son."

"Yes, madam," Ona said and went to fetch a bucket of water.

Madam Margaret prayed more than six times a day. Every Saturday, she washed the statue of the Mother of Christ holding her son which was in front of the church. She first placed a high stool near the statue. She fetched the bucket of water in which she threw in soap and a rag. She then climbed up the stool and proceeded to scrub the statue. She addressed the statue without mentioning the name of Maria, the mother of Jesus.

> *Jesus Christ, my son*
> *They have dirtied your face*
> *Never mind, my son*
> *Margaret has come*
> *To scrub it clean.*

> *Jesus Christ, my son*
> *They dirty your face*
> *Everyday*
> *The sinners among us*
> *Dirty your name*
> *Everyday.*

> *Jesus Christ, my son*
> *Those who crucified you*
> *On the cross*
> *Are burning even now*
> *In never quenching fire.*

> *Jesus Christ, my son*
> *They have dirtied your face*
> *Margaret is here*
> *To clean your face.*

The ritual amused Ona greatly. She was always happy to be asked to be a part of it. She wondered why Madam Margaret omitted the name of Maria, the mother of Jesus. She wondered whether this was a kind of discrimination on the part of Madam Margaret. When the ritual was over, Ona went back to the convent. She was as unhappy as ever. She was taught to pray and she learnt the catechism, but these did not affect her life in any way. She always wondered why her mother brought her to the convent. She resisted everything she was taught, including reading and writing. Her mind was always at home.

She did not eat most of the foods in the convent and when her mother did not bring her favorite foods, she went hungry. She became thin and was ill so frequently that her father went to the convent and, without permission, took her home.

Ona spent eighteen months in the convent. Her mother suggested that she go to school: "Let's send her to school."

"Was she not in school at the convent?" asked Mgbada.

"Not that type of school. I mean the regular school where her brothers and sister attend," said Akpe.

"I am afraid she is going to start rather late then. Her brothers and sister started at the age of seven. She is going to start at the age of thirteen. Yet, I don't mind her starting late. She can catch up if she desires. My problem is that she gives the impression that she is not interested in school."

"I think it is a good idea."

"She is something else, that child. And don't you wonder why I have not been pregnant ever since Ona was born?" Akpe complained.

Mgbada said nothing.

"Ona is thirteen years old."

"A child will come when it will come," said Mgbada. "But don't let that worry you"

"We have enough worries already. Let's face Ona's problems."

So, Ona went to school. But she was absent most of the time. When there were a few drops of rain, she refused to go to school, and nobody could persuade her to go. Because she was the youngest child, she was pampered. Her eldest brother wanted her to go to school and encouraged his brother and sister to make fun of her or sing with her name if she refused to go. They sang:

Ona, onye ujo akwukwo
Ona, onye ujo akwukwo
Ona is afraid of school
Ona is afraid of school.

But this did not make her want to go to school. The only errands she loved to do for her mother was fetching water and washing clothes in the Lake. Catching fish was what she loved to do at any time. True, she was discouraged by her mother to not go near water, but the fish she caught each time she went with her brothers and sister made her father insist that she must do what she had to do. Her grandmother, Nwafor, was a source of encouragement.

"My daughter," she said to her, "it is good to go to school. It is also good to be a good fisherwoman. God has given you that gift so make use of it. If you want to go to school, if school is going to change your life for the better, the same God will show you the way. You see, in this world we all have different destinies. Look at the lines on the palm of your hand; look at the lines on the palm of your sister's hand. They are not the same. No two pairs of palms have the same lines. That's the work of the Supreme God, and no one can alter it. I have told your mother not to worry you. You are destined for something big, something extraordinary. That's how I feel, my granddaughter."

Akpe fumed when she heard this. But there was nothing she could do other than report to her mother, who cautioned her to be patient because God was going to answer their prayers. Ona, she said, was going to be a good Christian worthy of her mother and grandmother. But Akpe was not consoled. She complained to her husband, who said to her:

"I have told you, you cannot stop this child from going to the water. It is not possible. Leave her to be herself. There must be something in that water. Leave her, perhaps in time she will find what she is looking for. I beg you. She is a mere child. This is only a phase, it will pass. She may forget with time. Let her be, I beg you. Don't let our children treat her unkindly. Don't let them think she is strange. Encourage them to treat her as their sister who has a peculiar problem. Ona is thin and fragile, but didn't you witness the blow she gave our eldest son when he was in her way the other day? That strength which she used on our son came from somewhere. I know you do not understand. One day you will understand."

Ona eventually dropped out of school. She helped her mother with her chores and in her sewing, while her brothers and sister went to school. She also spent her time fishing. In those days, women in Ugwuta used baskets to fish in Oruru, one of the streams that flowed into the Lake. Ona went to fish with members of her age-grade who did not go to school. The children sometimes spent a whole afternoon in Oruru catching fishes with their baskets.

Ona excelled in this pastime. It was said that she had cool hands which attracted fishes, for she sometimes used her bare hands to catch them. When she got home, she gave the fishes to her mother who grudgingly took them, made soup or dried them over the open fire. Other than that, Ona's childhood was sad and one could say she was unhappy. She kept to herself. She spoke only when spoken to. She played games by herself, talking to herself and imaginary children.

"What kind of child is this?" The people asked. "What a pity that God gave such a strange child to such good people. Sometimes, we don't deserve what we get in life. Akpe and Mgbada do not deserve to have such a strange child."

As if all these strange behaviors were not enough, Ona began to 'see.' She stopped people on the way and told them that she was sent to give them messages. She would proceed to deliver the messages. Some people stopped to hear the messages; some brushed her aside and went their way. Early one morning, one distraught woman knocked at Mgbada's door.

"Who is that?" Mgbada asked.

"It is me."

"Who are you?"

"It is me."

"Well, 'it is me' will open the door for you."

"Please, open the door. I have come to see your daughter."

"And you have no name? And my daughter has no name?"

"Please."

"Wait for the cock to crow… Go home, come back after cockcrow, my daughter is asleep. She is a mere child. Go home."

"Father, I know the voice, open the door."

"Ona, what are you doing here?"

"Father, please, I know the voice."

Mgbada opened the door, and the woman entered. Akpe had prepared to go for morning mass; nothing would stop her from going, so she left.

"Sit down," Mgbada said, "while I wash my face and hands. Ona, come and sit with her." The woman stared at Ona. She opened her mouth to talk, but no words came out.

Ona sat down calmly waiting for her father to return. In front of the house, Mgbada crouched in front of a bowl of water and before he washed his hands and face, he said:

> *Our ancestors*
> *I greet you*

I thank you for waking us up
This morning
We are good people
We are peaceful people
We do not harm anybody
If anyone wishes to harm us
May you harm him first
If anyone wishes to kill us
May you kill him first

Our ancestors
Here is my daughter
You know why she chose us
You alone know her mission
We are mere mortals
May her mission be good
May her mission be beneficial
To all of us in our clan
Our ancestors
We know you protect us
You know why this woman has come
Deal with her
If she brought evil to us
Spare her
If she brought good

Our ancestors

Here is kola nut
Here is kai kai
To you and to us
Our ancestors
We greet you.

Mgbada washed his hands and face, dried them with a towel and went into the room. He cleared his throat and sat down. He broke the kola nut and gave the visitor a lobe, and said,

"You have come to see my daughter?"
"Yes."
"Why have you come?"
"My daughter died."
"Died?"
"Yes, she died."
"Go on."
"My daughter died."
"You want my daughter to resurrect her?"
"No."
"Go and bury her then."
"I have buried her."
"What do you want my daughter to do for you?"
"She warned me."
"Yes?"
"I did not understand."
"Go on, I am listening."

"It was on Afo, I remember the day very clearly. I was returning from Afo Ugbani; I was heavy with child. Your daughter stopped me and began to talk, but…"

"You did not want to hear her?"

"Yes, I was impatient. The load on my head was heavy. The child inside me was kicking, so I wasn't really paying attention to her. But I thought I heard her say, 'Your baby will die if you do not sacrifice a white ram to the Woman of the Lake.' Then I heard someone say, 'This child has come again-*o-o*, this child who has refused to go to school. This child who is afraid of school. This child who is the daughter of Mgbada, the teacher of my children. What is Mgbada doing about this strange child?'"

"I have said it all. I went my way. I forgot all that your daughter said to me. Soon I had my baby; exactly twenty-eight days later, my baby died. Then I remembered what she said. I have buried my daughter. I have gone to the Lake and dipped my feet in water. I have come to see your daughter."

"Welcome. Ona, what do you say?"

"She should do what I asked her to do before she gives birth to a baby."

"Is that all?"

"That's all."

"You have heard."

"I have."

"Go and sacrifice a white ram to the Lake Goddess."

Chapter 8

"Have you heard the news?" said Ekecha.

"What news?" asked Mgbeke.

"You don't seem to be a part of this town. Haven't you heard that Ona, the daughter of Akpe and Mgbada has got married?"

"Married? Ona?" exclaimed Mgbeke.

"Ona indeed."

"To whom?"

"That is the question, to whom?"

"Hey wonders will never cease! Ona the mad one? Hey, God, are you there? Do you hear? If that one found a man to marry her, then my daughter will also find a husband. Tell me, my sister, to whom? You are right, I am never at home. Work will kill me. There are four days in the week. On Nkwo, I go to the market here in Ugwuta; on Eke, I go to Eke Mgbidi; on Orie, I go to Omuma; on Afo, I go to Afo Ugbani. On Nkwo again…"

"What can we do, my dear sister? We have to keep body and soul together. If you have a husband, it is the same thing. If you don't have, it is worse," said Ekecha.

"You are right, my sister, but tell me, how many husbands in Ugwuta give their wives house-keeping money? How many? I can count them on my ten fingers." She proceeded to count: "There is George Ogbuzuru; he works with the U.A.C. as a clerk. His wife went to school. He was known to be stingy. When they got married, his wife stopped teaching. She sews at home. There is," she continued, "Louis Okoronkwo who works with the G.B. Ollivant. His wife did not go to school like me, but she stays at home and Louis feeds her and the children," Mgbeke concluded.

"That's what I am saying, married or not a woman must work hard."

"And also, Lawrence Ossai who works with John Holts; the one who constantly beats his wife."

The women roared with laughter.

"She does not go to the market at all. Lawrence forbids her to go to market. If a piece of *george* costs two pounds, he buys it for his wife."

"You mean it?"

"It is true, when I was dealing in *george*, any time I had a new design, I took it to Lawrence and he bought it for his wife."

"And he paid cash?"

"He paid cash. He is not one of those who will tell you to come for your money at month's end," said Ekecha.

"That is good. We have counted three. How many more?"

"About three or four. That's all."

"So, you see, we have to work hard, all women must work hard, husband or no husband, I repeat."

"But tell me, who married Akpe's mad daughter?"

"I don't know. They say he is a foreigner," replied Ekecha.

"He must be a foreigner to marry that one. My sister, I know that to get a husband, I mean a good husband, is difficult these days, but I am not going to allow my daughter to marry a foreigner. Will you?" asked Mgbeke.

"Not me. A foreigner? No way. The husband of my daughter must be born in this town. His parents, and I mean both parents, must be natives of this town."

"But you can understand why Akpe allowed it?"

"I understand. Tell me, what part of Igboland does the man come from?"

"I don't know, but I suspect he is from the Orlu area."

"God forbid, Orlu area? Not even Onitsha area? Ogbuide forbid! What a pity! I am sorry for Akpe."

"Don't be sorry for her; she is happy with the marriage. The man, I hear, is well-to-do. He paid a handsome bride wealth, too."

"You don't mean it."

"And when I say a handsome bride wealth, I mean a handsome one."

"Is that so?"

"Yes, for that strange, mad girl who refused to go to school like her brothers and sister. Didn't our people say that the dog with a tail says that human beings, blessed with buttocks, do not know how to sit. Foolish girl. She has parents who can send her to school and she refused to go. If I had had parents who could send me to school, I would have been educated. I would have married a clerk, or even a manager. I wouldn't be suffering as I am suffering now, going to all these markets, carrying load to and fro."

"I could have gone," added her companion, "If I was interested, but I was not. I preferred to trade. Tell me, what have I got to show for it now? I have been trading since I was twelve years old. If I had gone to school, I could have married well. I would lack nothing."

"I am not sure about lacking nothing. Remember what it means to just sit at home and take care of the children; cook for your husband when he brings the money of course, do exactly as he wants you to do. I don't know whether I would enjoy that kind of life."

"I will enjoy it. Who wants to suffer? Don't you envy the wives of these clerks and managers? I envy them."

"I must be truthful; I envy them too. But they envy us as we envy them."

"I don't believe you. What do I have that such women will envy?"

"Those women you envy have their own problems."

"Every woman has her own problems, I know."

"Their husbands do a lot of things."

"Like what?"

"Like bringing women into the home."

"Don't our husbands do the same?"

"They don't, you know they don't."

"Well, I know what you mean. There is only one bedroom, so where will our husbands take other women to…?" Both women began to laugh.

"Jokes aside," continued one of the women, "Those women you envy don't have easy lives. The so-called respectable husbands beat them at the slightest provocation."

"I know who you mean," said the other, and she went on. "The woman is a relation of mine. Her husband was rather free with women. But she consoled herself by saying that as long as her husband did not bring the women into her home; it was all right by her. So, one night, her husband brought home a woman; she pretended that she was sleeping. When her husband finished with the woman, he woke his wife up and ordered her to go to the kitchen and cook for them. She told him that she was tired and that besides there was no fish in the house. Thereupon, he pounced on her

and began to beat her. She did not resist. The woman—
that is, the mistress—began to beg him not to beat his
wife, but he ignored her. When the beating was too
much, the wife went to the kitchen, took a heavy object
or something, and landed it on her husband's head and
blood gushed out. The mistress disappeared. The wife
went to bed, leaving him to bleed. She did not go for
help; she did not shout for help. Next day, the husband
took his wife back to her father, saying, 'Take your
daughter, she ceases to be my wife from today.'

'Wait and eat kola with me, my son, please,' pleaded
the father-in-law. But his son-in-law had gone. The old
man turned to his daughter: 'What did you do? Did he
catch you with a man?' The old man persuaded her to
talk, but no words came out. When her mother returned,
she took her daughter into the room and questioned her.
She told her mother exactly what happened. When she
finished, her mother asked her what her plans were.
She had no plans. 'If you have no plans, go back to your
husband. You have children, what will become of your
children? You do not know what life is all about, what
marriage is all about. Husbands have done worse things
to their wives. You are no exception, *di bu nma ogori*, the
beauty of a damsel is recognized only when she has a
husband. So, swallow your pride and go back to your
husband. You don't belong here anymore, so please go
back to your husband.' Her mother went to her son-in-

law and after a long discussion the rejected wife went back to her husband."

"Didn't the wife tell her mother what actually happened?"

"She did."

"That's serious."

"That's very serious. I will not take it from anybody."

"Me, neither."

"Not even if he gives me a hundred pounds a month."

"Me, neither."

"It is sad."

"That's what I mean. You and I who have not gone to school cannot take it. But here are our fellow women, who went to school, who have their so-called pieces of paper which can earn them money, behaving as if they have no pride, as if they have no homes to go to. Me, I will pack my bag and baggage and go back to my father's house. Then I will proceed to marry another husband ten times better than the previous one."

"Nonsense, is he the only one with a penis?"

"I wonder," and the women laughed uproariously and slapped each other's back.

"You know this is my second marriage."

"Of course, I know."

"Two or three months after our marriage, my husband began to return home very late. So, when he did it three or four times, I called him, I said to him, 'I know what you are doing, and I know whom you are doing it with. What you are looking for outside, I have it right here. If you cannot or will not buy mine, I am going to sell it right under your nose to the highest bidder. I will sell it in such a way that you will beg me.' So... Nobody told him what to do after this. He behaved himself. But these women who went to school and married these so-called educated men behave as if their husbands are the only ones that have penises. I cannot understand it. I know how to care for a man, but he must give me the respect that is due to me, otherwise I paddle my own canoe."

Ona got married to a man who traded in Ugwuta. He was not a very rich man but he was well-to-do. The man, Mr. Sylvester—that was the name he was known by everybody in Ugwuta and environs—was a good and practicing Christian and that was what pleased Akpe in the first place. She was excited and so was her mother, Mama Theresa. Their prayers had been answered. Didn't they believe in God? God was great. God had brought to their doorstep a man of God to marry their daughter. Mr. Sylvester had seen Ona with other children in the beach market. She had come to help a woman sell palm kernel since she was no longer interested in sewing with her mother. He had taken to her immediately and had made inquiries. Since he was a church member, he made inquiries from the church. Nobody told Mr. Sylvester Ona's history, nobody told him about her numerous disappearances and her strange ways. Likewise, Ona's parents knew next to nothing about Mr. Sylvester, except that he was a trader and a Christian.

There was excitement on both sides. The only one who was not excited was Ona. She seemed to not know what it was all about. Her parents and the two grandmothers told her that it was the best thing that had ever happened to her since her birth. Who was she to doubt these important people in her life? They told her that her husband was rich and would take good care of her. They told her she would wear a white flowing wedding gown on her wedding day, and that there would be feasting and rejoicing on that day. They told her she was going to be a mother, but that her three mothers were going to bend over backwards to see that all went well with her. They would take it in turns to look after her and her babies. They did not tell her what she must do in order to have these babies. But she was excited, too, when she saw all the fuss the grown-ups were making over her.

For the first time in the family of Mgbada everyone was relaxed. The children were happy that Ona was going to marry after all. They had heard their parents discuss this many nights. They knew how anxious their mother was about Ona and how she had fasted and chanted "Hail Mary" for her daughter. Indeed, God answers prayers, the children concluded. Ona's parents believed that once she was married, the evil spirit would leave her and she would not be able to 'see' any more. She was a virgin. Once she knew a man, they believed, she would lose the power to 'see.' Akpe was not the only one who believed this; Mgbada also believed. He knew that if one wanted to foretell fortunes or see far beyond the comprehension of other mortals, he had to be pure, had to abstain from sexual activities and had to fast. Both parents were going to make the church wedding the best in the history of Ugwuta. Nwafor and Mama Theresa swung into action. They used all the resources available to them to make the wedding a huge success, and it was indeed a huge success. The three mothers and their relations filled boxes with *george* materials, jewelry of all kinds, especially coral beads and agate stones. It was at this time that Nwafor realized that her namesake did not, in fact, sell her coral beads. Cooking utensils, plates, basins of all sizes, buckets, cups, glasses, even brooms were given to Ona for her new home. The people marveled at the things that were given to her. Even her husband was amazed. His people did not do this. He was happy that he had made a good choice. He did not marry a poor man's daughter.

After the wedding, Ona, accompanied by her people, went to her new home with the gifts from her parents.

When her age-grade began to sing the goodbye song, "Ona, goodbye, there is no going back," She burst into tears and tore the veil and began to weep hysterically. The weeping took everybody by surprise. Ona did not just cry openly, she wailed.

"This girl is going to disgrace us," said Akpe. "Mgbada, don't you know what to do? Console her; I am sure she will listen to you. Tell her you are taking her home and not to her husband's home," continued Akpe.

It worked. Mgbada came closer, gently brushed aside the bridegroom and wiped his daughter's tears with his handkerchief and said, "My daughter, why are you crying? Nobody will hurt you. Not this man beside you while I am here. Wipe your tears, we shall go home now. I am taking you back to your father's house. Now, my son-in-law," he turned to Mr. Sylvester, "You have to go home without your bride. But leave everything to me. She will be with you today. You can see she is a mere child, and we, her parents, are to blame for over pampering her."

What could the man do?

Mgbada took Ona back home. Members of her age-grade followed, but they did not sing. When they arrived home, Akpe gave them some presents and they dispersed. Mgbada took Ona to his room; persuaded her to change her clothes and she reluctantly did. Her favorite dish—*mbaze* with prawns—was prepared. She ate and soon fell asleep, for she was tired. While she slept, her father carried her to her husband's house. She slept on. In the middle of the night, she woke up to the strange room, and she remembered. She wept softly. Her husband who had not slept wiped her tears. When she stopped weeping, he took her, knew her and broke her virginity. She was sixteen.

Chapter 9

Mgbeke and Ekecha were fish-sellers. They had gone early to Urashi River to wait for fishermen who went to fish at night. They were lucky for they bought two large fishes, *asa* and *atuma*, for only two pounds; fishes they could sell in the market for four pounds.

Nkwo market was filling up with people when Mgbeke and Ekecha arrived there. There were hundreds of stalls; men and women, boys and girls, young and old were in the market with their wares. All sorts of assorted goods—bottles, oranges, groundnuts, palm oil, palm kernel, yams, cassava, cocoyam, bitter-leaf, corn flour, etc. People milled around aimlessly, talking to one another, moving, stopping and moving on. Some shouted obscenities to no one in particular. The beggars and mad people were not left out.

Mad Eziti on this particular Nkwo surpassed herself. Normally she tied a small piece of cloth round her waist—just long enough to cover her nakedness. Today, she was different. She wore a well-tailored *up and down* print, which fitted her tiny body. She had on a soft multicolored head-tie. She had a bath. Often, she did not bathe. So, she was unusually clean. She had a long chewing stick in her mouth. She chewed away and spat out the saliva, making a hissing sound like that of a snake.

"Who is that?" the voice showed displeasure.

"Mad Eziti, of course. Can't you see?" said Mgbeke.

"No, she is not the one. Look at her properly."

"I saw her before you. She is the mad Eziti."

"Who gave her the clothes she is wearing?"

"A relative, perhaps."

"She has relations?"

"She has relations, mad people do have relations. Don't blame them, they tried."

"She is to blame, then."

"Do I know?"

"Eziti, I am greeting you."

Mad Eziti turned around and said, "Our Mgbeke, you have come to the market."

"I am greeting you, too," said Ekecha.

"I didn't see you."

"Eziti, it is me, Ekecha."

"I know that it is Ekecha greeting me. But I have not seen her. I have only seen Mgbeke. Mgbeke, my sister, how are you?"

"I am fine. My friend is greeting you. Why don't you answer her?"

"Why should I? She did not create me. I am to blame for being mad."

"*Ewoo*, Eziti, you heard?"

"I am mad, but I am not deaf."

"Don't worry. I like your dress."

"A mad woman's dress?"

"I said, forget that. Tell me, are we going to be lucky today?"

"Ogbuide herself will buy your fish today."

"Really?"

"I am mad, but I speak the truth. I saw Ogbuide this morning. She is coming to the market and she is going to buy your fish."

"Why are you listening to a mad woman?"

"Ekecha, please, she will hear you."

"I heard her, don't worry." Mad Eziti went on chewing her stick as if her whole life depended on it. "Have you seen mad Ose over there?" she asked.

"No."

"He is overturning the tables of market women. He is destroying their wares. I don't like his brand of madness."

"His brand?"

"His brand. There are different kinds of madness. Mine, for instance, is the good one. I don't beat people.

If I beg you for food or money and you don't give me any, I leave you. If you give me something, I thank you and go my way. But Ose is something else. He is violent. I hate violence… Run. He is coming here. He is shouting. Stupid mad man, that's not how to be mad. Come here let me teach you the art of madness. Foolish man."

Ose was stark naked. He carried a big stick. He was tall and gaunt. He looked athletic and rather handsome. His chest was hairy. His hair was long and twisted like ropes. His eyes were sharp, red, twinkling like stars. He had a perfect erection which made the women run for safety. Eziti stood in defiance, ignoring all of Ose's show of force.

"You foolish woman. Why don't you want to marry me?"

"You mad man, why should I marry you? You are mad, you are naked. Can't you see me? Can't you see my clothes? Can't you see how respectable I am? Look at yourself—that's not how to be mad."

"Teach me the art of madness then. You witch."

"Who is a witch?"

"You."

"Me?"

"You."

"Now, you are going to see a witch. I am going to bewitch you now."

Eziti proceeded to remove her clothes. The market women shouted in protest, "Eziti no, Eziti no."

The market women and men shook their heads. "Madness is bad," they said. The idle children in the market surged forward to have a clearer view of the two mad people who were about to give them free entertainment. The old people drove the children away. By this time, Eziti had been persuaded not to undress. Ose had moved away brandishing his stick, causing havoc as he went along.

"This is Nkwo market for you," said Mgbeke.

"Ogbuide will soon come to the market."

Mgbeke smiled and said, "Don't dismiss it as a mad woman's talk. You will see. These mad people sometimes see what we don't see."

"Because they talk to themselves?"

"Partly that. They see things that we don't see."

"Ghosts?"

"Spirits."

"Witches."

"Ancestors."

"They see and don't see."

More fish-sellers joined Ekecha and Mgbeke. They began to compare notes.

"Where did you buy yours?"

"On the mouth of Urashi River. Do you like them?"

"They are good. But not as fresh as ours."

"That's a lie."

"It is no lie, look at our fishes," said the other.

"When did you get to Urashi River?"

"Before the cock crew."

"You went before us, so you missed the fishes that we bought," Mgbeke said.

"Mgbeke, let's leave this place. These miserable fish-sellers will give us bad luck."

"Who will give who bad luck? Ekecha, your other name is bad luck. Do you want me to tell you? Eh?"

"Mgbeke, come, let's go to another part of the market. Yes, my other name is bad luck. So, I must now carry my bad luck with me. I am leaving you and your good luck. Good luck to you and your smelling, rotten fishes."

"You say my fishes are rotten?"

"Your fishes are rotten. Can't you smell? Miserable fish-seller."

"Who said my fishes are rotten, eh?"

"Come, let's go, Mgbeke."

Mgbeke and Ekecha moved to another part of the market where they thought it was quieter. But they were greeted by angry women who were driving away a hoard of beggars. Very glaring were the sores on some of the beggars' legs, and the flies that followed them.

"Nkwo market is no longer Nkwo market," lamented Ekecha.

"What part of the country would you say these ones came from?"

"Up country. Where else?"

"The sores smell. We can't sell our fishes here."

"Where do we go next?"

"Over there."

"Where there are baskets of cassava. How can Ogbuide, our mother, come to that part of the market? She hates cassava and its smell. We have to go back to our rightful place."

They went back. They ignored their fellow fish-sellers, put down their basin of fishes and waited. Their first customer was Mrs. George Ogbuzuru. She wanted to buy one of the fishes, but was told that the two must be sold together.

"How much are they then?" asked Mrs. Ogbuzuru.

"They are expensive," replied one of the fish-sellers.

Mrs. Ogbuzuru ignored the insult... and asked again, "How much are you selling your fishes?"

"Ten pounds."

"Are you selling a cow?"

"Perhaps what you see in that basin is a cow. We sell what you see in that basin—two fishes—and they cost ten pounds. And please, if you don't have enough money to buy the fishes, leave us alone. You are our first customer. Don't bring us bad luck."

"You are the ones who want to give me bad luck this Nkwo morning."

"We don't want you to have our bad luck, so leave

us. We know you don't buy this kind of fish. Off you go. Take your good luck with you."

"If they sent you to me this morning, you smelling fish-sellers, tell them that you have not seen me. What exactly are you selling? Not fish? What is swelling your heads? Fish? You…"

"Hold it, you what? You…?" She had untied her head-tie and tied it on her waist, a signal that she was ready to fight.

"Mgbeke, leave her to me. Come Mrs., Mrs. for nothing. You want us to tell you what is swelling our heads? Do you really want to know? Well, what is swelling our heads is poverty. Do you hear? Poverty. I am drunk with poverty. I have told you, leave us or I will pour fish water on you."

"Mrs. Ogbuzuru, what is the matter?" asked Mrs. Ossai.

"*Ewoo!*" exclaimed Ekecha.

"They are all here today. White women whose mothers are black. Our fellow women who don't suffer like we do. You have come to buy, too, on Nkwo. Good. I hope your husbands gave you plenty of money to spend on our fishes. If you don't have enough money, please go back to them and ask for more."

"You think we envy you?" continued the other woman. "We work hard, we earn every penny, and we spend the money the way we like. We give account to no one."

"And you can see that it is fish that we are selling, not cow. We sell the two for ten pounds," Mgbeke said.

"Our Mgbeke, what is the matter?" asked Mrs. Ossai again. She was used to the two women and their big, bad mouths. But by this time, Mrs. Ogbuzuru had left the women saying to them, "Sell your fish. You are nothing but fish-sellers."

"You lie, Mrs., you lie. Look at you, the wife of a rich man. Don't you see how thin you look? What do you do with all the money your husband gives you? Get out of here, you can't buy this kind of fish. Go to where they sell dry fish. That's what you usually buy. Come, my sister."

Turning to Mrs. Ossai, she said, "If you want to buy our fish, buy. Don't worry yourself about the broken one who looks like soup without fish."

"Mgbeke, it's enough. Why are you quarrelling this morning, Nkwo morning, of all mornings?" asked Mrs. Ossai.

"Don't mind that one. We gave her the price of our fish and she asked us if we were selling a cow. A cow! Didn't she have eyes to see that it was fish we were selling? If her husband was miserly, should she take it out on us?"

"Is that all? Is that not enough to spoil one's day? Nkwo morning of all mornings?"

"Don't worry. She has gone now. She did not mean

any harm. I like your fish. They are fresh. How much are they?"

"Thank you, my sister. Whether you buy or not, I am happy. I am satisfied that you have praised our fish. You know a good fish when you see one. The fisherman caught them a few minutes before we arrived on the scene. We bought them and asked him to kill them because we were afraid that they might jump into the water. Buy them for ten pounds."

"The fishes are fresh, but they are expensive."

"How much do you want to buy them?"

"I am going to pay nine pounds."

"Good market."

"Eight pounds."

"Good market."

"Seven."

"Market."

"Give me the fishes for three pounds ten shillings."

"Have you finished?"

"Yes."

"Let me tell you something. When I have something good to sell, I hate to sell it to someone I do not like. That was why I did not want Mrs. Ogbuzuru to buy our fish. Look at her. See how thin she is, with all the money her husband gives her and her children."

"It is enough, our Mgbeke. I am in a hurry. I have other things to buy. I like your fish. Give them to me for four pounds."

"Is that your last offer?"

"Yes."

"No, we shall not sell. Our gain is only ten shillings if we sell the fishes to you for seven pounds. I am telling you the truth. In the name of God, in the name of my dead mother, I am telling you the truth. In the name of God who created me, I am…"

"*Ewoo*, it is enough, save your breath."

"Mrs. Mgbeke is telling you the truth. Make another offer. We did not buy them for seven pounds. We know the kind of fish that your husband eats, make another offer."

"I am not going any further."

"All right, go well. But you can see that fish is scarce in the market."

"I know. There is time."

"Buy the fish now. You will regret it if you don't buy it now."

"Four pounds and ten shillings. Are you selling to me or not?"

"Wait for more fishes to be brought to the market. There is time."

At this juncture another woman came. She must have been eavesdropping: "Mgbeke and Ekecha, your fishes are fresh and good. But Mrs. Ossai has priced them well. Why don't you sell them to her?"

"My sister, who invited you now? Do you buy this

kind of fish? Do you know how much they cost? Please go your way and don't put your mouth into something that does not concern you. What kind of Nkwo is this?"

The woman thus addressed smiled.

"I know you Mgbeke, and you Ekecha. Sell the fishes to Mrs. Ossai; who else will buy them? Father's cook has bought. Mrs. Kaiser has bought. You want to take the trouble of drying them this rainy season? Where will you buy dry firewood? Sell the fishes now."

"Please go your way, I beg you," said Ekecha.

As for Mgbeke, she eyed the woman in such a way that she could have melted away. "The people of this town don't call a spade what it is, a spade. If you don't have money, like me, why don't you say so? Ekecha, don't mind them. We are going to sell these fishes for eight pounds. You wait. If we don't sell them today, we shall dry them. Suffering is my second name. I am going to suffer to dry the fishes, but I am not going to sell them for four pounds ten shillings. You will see, our Mother will come to the market and buy our fish. We are going to make money today. Come and buy fresh fish. Come here and buy. A good market sells itself. Come and buy!" Mgbeke shouted.

"The best fish from the Lake is here. Come and buy!" Ekecha shouted.

They made some provocative dance steps, annoying their fellow fish-sellers. But they were completely ignored. Shortly after, Ona came to buy fish. She looked well-fed. She had changed dramatically for the better. She no longer looked timid and frightened as she did before her marriage to Mr. Sylvester. It was said that marriage suited her, and that she should have been married off years ago. She had bought most of the things she wanted to buy. Mgbeke and Ekecha had seen her before the other fish-sellers and called her to buy their fish. But the other fish-sellers almost dragged her to their own basin of fish.

"But we called her first," protested Mgbeke. The fish-sellers were silent. "Ona, leave their rotten fishes and come over and buy ours. Ekecha, we must not quarrel today. Ona, do you hear? We know your husband does not eat those kinds of fishes."

"Mgbeke and Ekecha, if I open my mouth and talk to you today, I am not the daughter of my mother."

"Look, look, look at her. Who is your mother, eh?"

"Her mother sold fish like us and never one day gave the age-grade *kai kai* to drink."

"And what have you done since she died, eh?"

"You are so poor you have not given her a second burial."

"So be quick and do so before she gets angry and strikes you dead from the spirit world."

True to her word, the fish-seller did not reply. Instead, she spat on the ground.

"Ona, have you seen the fish? Come over here and see ours."

Ona was tactful. She moved away from the fish-sellers, and the 'eye' war began among the women. Mgbeke and Ekecha eyed the other fish-sellers in an evil way. While contorting their faces, they gazed at the fish-sellers from head to toe and ended up spitting on the ground. There were no verbal exchanges, no physical contact, only the eyes were used for this kind of fight. When they were tired, Mgbeke made some provocative dance steps to annoy the fish-sellers. When they finished the fight, Ekecha said, "Ona does not look at all bad."

"Yes, she looks great."

"She is very beautiful."

"She has always been beautiful."

"Her husband, I hear, takes very good care of her."

"So I hear. Lucky girl."

"He is a trader."

"A trader who deals in medicines."

"In medicines?"

"The white man's medicines."

"That's understandable because Mgbada is a medicine man."

"Yes, and a diviner as well."

"That's a wonderful combination."

"Yes, one complements the other."

"She is coming back."

"We must sell our fishes to her. Leave me to do the talking. I know how to deal with her,"

Mgbeke cleared her throat, untied and retied her *wrappa* tightly around her waist and welcomed Ona thus:

"Haa Ona. Our little, beautiful Mrs., welcome to the market. How are you? Lovely girl. I have not seen your mother for some time now. I hope she is well. And your grandmother? You are looking gorgeous, our little girl. Your husband must be taking great care of you. Good. That's how it should be. Try and have a bouncing baby boy for him. Do you hear? You have come to buy fish. We have good fishes. We always sell fresh and delicious fish; the one that your husband would like. We hear he loves fresh fish."

She tilted the basin of fish for Ona to take a better look.

"You see how fresh they are."

"How much is the big one?" asked Ona.

"We sell the two together. We…"

"Ekecha, no. Ona, the big one is five… What is wrong with you children, eh? Why don't you look where you are going? Do you want to push your mothers down, eh? Take your plaything and run. You shouldn't be playing in the market. Run."

One of the children thus addressed said, "Mama, give us fish."

"Give you fish?"

"Yes," said the other child.

The children were naked and dirty, their noses were running. One licked the mucus with his tongue as he spoke. "Don't, don't, wait, let me wipe your nose for you," Mgbeke said as she took hold of the child's neck and wiped his nose with the tip of her *wrappa*. Without saying thank you, the child yelled out again, "Give us fish."

"*Ugwuta-ee*, who sent you to us this Nkwo morning?"

"Are you spirit children?"

"Ogbuide sent us," the children said simultaneously. "We have come to the market today."

"Ogbuide sent you to us?"

"Yes."

"Give us fish or money."

"We shall bring to you children from the spirit world," said another child.

"Do you hear what I am hearing?"

"We have not sold anything. You can see the two big fishes in the basin. We cannot give them to you."

"Give us money," they demanded.

"Here, take this." Ona gave them a brand new sixpence.

"God bless you. Ogbuide bless you." They ran away.

Mgbeke shouted: "Come back, come back."

They came back. "Take this." Mgbeke gave them a

penny. She spoke to Ekecha: "Are you a fool? Give them something before they disappear. Don't you know that Ogbuide comes to the market in different forms?"

Ekecha gave them a penny.

"God bless you," the children chorused and disappeared into the market.

For a long time, Ona did not move. When she recovered, she heaved a sigh of relief and faced the women. "I want to buy one of the fishes."

"We sell all…"

"No, Ekecha, let her buy one if she wants to. Ona, you can buy one. Give us ten pounds."

"They are good fishes."

"They are."

"But expensive."

"Good things are expensive."

"Price the fish."

"It is the *asa* that I want."

"Go ahead and make an offer."

"I don't know."

"Make an offer. We won't eat you."

Ona looked at the fish again. She could see one of the boys who begged for money a while ago. She remained silent. Then again she could see Idenu's head replace the fish's head in the basin. She shook her head violently. The women looked on in astonishment. The other fish-sellers watched the quiet drama, and waited, then one of them said: "Come over here if they have bewitched you."

Ona recovered, smiled and said, "Idenu, I am not happy about Idenu."

"Your sister?"

"Yes."

"Why?"

"She does not want to stay."

"What do you mean?"

Ona was silent. Then she said, "Sell the fish to me for three pounds."

Mgbeke was confused. She heard Ekecha saying: "Make another offer. Add more money. We shall cut up the fish nicely for you."

"My last offer is three pounds ten shillings."

Mgbeke recovered. Ona opened her bag and brought out the money.

Ekecha began to cut up the fish vigorously, saying: "What can we do? It is bad market. Ona, it is just because of you that we are selling this fish for three pounds ten shillings. Someone offered four pounds ten shillings and we refused. Foolish me. I refused. Now we are losing one pound." She went on, expertly cutting up the fish, "You can see how fresh the blood is. You are lucky."

Ona left.

"You see how Ogbuide operates?"

"She came in two forms: the children and Ona.

Those children, there was something about them. Did you look at them well?"

"I did."

"I looked at them very well. There's something about them. They did not beg. They were not beggars. They were demanding something from us. Fish or money. Fish or money. That's not how to beg. They must have been sent purposely to us."

"You think so?"

"I think so. You know I am not by nature superstitious. There was something in the eyes of the children."

"We have not passed childbearing age. So perhaps they brought us children, "Ekecha said lightly.

She went on, "Ogbuide has broken kola nuts for us. Three pounds ten shillings for one fish. We have already made a profit of one pound ten shillings. Ona's husband must have plenty of money. These foreigners make good husbands. Mgbeke, we can go home now."

"Mm?"

"I said, we can go home now."

"Without selling this one?"

"We can eat it."

"Say that again."

"Eat it, I said."

"That's why you are poor. Look at your mouth. The mouth you will use in eating three pounds ten shillings fish. Eat it indeed. Do you have yams or cassava? Have you bought pepper and salt? Or are you going to boil the fish in water? Even if you do, do you have firewood? Poverty is bad. God, listen to me. In my next world, God, don't make me poor. God, I am going to be a rich woman. My mother will be rich, my father will be rich. I am going to be rich. My husband will be rich. I shall lack nothing. God, do you hear me?"

"Mgbeke, it is enough, what is the matter? It is enough."

"It is not enough, you poor fish-seller," Mgbeke said.

The other fish-sellers enjoyed the drama, but they were silent. They had watched everything and they were green with envy, for they had not sold their fishes. It was dawning on them that they could not sell their fish until Mgbeke and Ekecha sold theirs. They sighted the Father's cook. "Come and buy our fish, Father's cook."

Some Rev. Sisters had arrived at the Mission and were hungry and wanted to eat fresh fish from Ugwuta. So, the cook was sent to the market. The forty-year-old cook went to the other fish-sellers, saw their fishes, shook his head and went over to Mgbeke and Ekecha.

"You see what you caused?" said one fish-seller to the other.

"What did I cause?"

"You were sleeping like a lazy white woman."

"I woke up in time. You were the one who changed the venue without informing me." The fish-seller hissed, sprinkled the fishes with fresh water and waited.

"Cook, buy our fish," said Ekecha.

"How much?"

"That's more like it; *ndi afia* how much?"

"Six pounds."

"Four pounds," offered the cook.

"No."

"Four pounds ten shillings."

"No."

"Yes, bring money." Ekecha brushed Mgbeke aside and proceeded to cut up the fish.

"You are lucky," said Mgbeke, "my friend has given you ten shillings. Pay money."

The cook paid and left.

"We must run before those poor people over there shoot us dead with their hungry, wicked eyes."

"They should not worry; their luck would be next time. These things go round."

Mgbeke and Ekecha went home. They shared their profits. Mgbeke brought some *kai kai* for them to drink and as they drank they talked:

"She is pregnant."

"Who?"

"Ona. She is four months pregnant."

"That is right. I wanted to say it, to ask you, but I

was not sure. There is clear evidence. I am happy for her and her mother."

"So am I. But she is a strange child. A very strange child."

"I agree with you. She does not like her sister very much."

"Idenu?"

"Yes, Idenu."

"Really. And she said that Idenu did not want to stay."

"She said so. Perhaps her sister is one of those children who are born to punish their parents."

"And being a strange child with some supernatural powers, she knows."

"I have no patience for such children. I remember when we were children, I witnessed a father butcher his dead son."

"No."

"The son was one of such children. The father had marked him when he died. He came back again. His father recognized him by the mark he gave him. He refused to treat him well, and when he eventually died, his father cut him up in pieces before he buried him. His subsequent children lived."

"Our world is strange. And sometimes when the children returned with the marks their parents gave them, it was said that they had been rejected by their spirit parents in the spirit world."

"Ona knows that her sister is one of them."

"Mgbada should also know, he is a medicine man."

"And a diviner, too."

"Yes, but sometimes—and that's why our world is strange—sometimes those who should know do not know."

"I do not dispute the fact. I think I should tell Akpe about Idenu."

"You must. You know her better than I do."

"They say Ona is possessed by *agwu*"

"I think it is Ogbuide herself who is troubling her. And unless something is done, she will never be a normal person."

"Now that she is married?"

"Even with a husband, yes. Her husband cannot compete with Ogbuide. No mortal can compete with a deity as powerful as Ogbuide."

"So, what do you think will happen?"

"Ogbuide will triumph in the end."

"You mean that Ona will eventually leave her husband?"

"She will. Her husband would be so harassed by the forces surrounding Ogbuide that he would run away. He will abandon Ona."

"Our world is strange."

"Very strange."

"And there is nothing anyone can do?"

"All Ona's parents can do is to allow her to worship Ogbuide, for she has chosen her. Ogbuide is powerful, you know, she is very jealous, too. You have to serve her and her alone. She is very demanding as well. I don't envy Ona at all."

"What a pity. Our world is strange. Look at Akpe and look at her mother, Mama Theresa—such good people. And they are Christians, too. Why doesn't Ogbuide call me to worship her?"

"You don't mean what you are saying. Fancy you being called to worship the great woman."

"You think I cannot be called? That I am not worthy?"

"Leave it at that, my friend. Only special people are called."

"And I am not special?"

"I said, leave it at that. You and I cannot be called. We are not special people. How can our Ogbuide call fish-sellers like us?" Both women laughed and Ekecha continued, "You think you can forsake all and worship her?"

"You mean leave my husband?"

"Well, yes and no. Some women that I know who are priestesses of Ogbuide have all passed childbearing age. So, it does not matter at all. But look at that child, Ona. How old is she? She is a mere child. The call is too early, that is, if it is indeed a call, and not madness. I don't think I would like my daughter to be called at that age, even at an older age."

"I would like to be called late in life, like Efuru was called," said Mgbeke.

"Efuru, the good one, the daughter of Nwashike Ogene?"

"Who else? She was called late in life," continued Mgbeke, "after suffering indignities from her husbands. What else was left for her to do than be the priestess of Ogbuide? That's the time to be called. Efuru performed very well."

"Really, I didn't know her."

"You didn't know her?"

"No. I was at Ose Akwa with my mother at the time she was the priestess of Ogbuide."

"You missed something. She gave dignity to the whole cult. She was the leader and every member of the cult from far and near respected her. She was always calm; always spoke in a slow and measured tone. She never raised her voice. She did not claim to do what she had no power to do."

"She never married again?"

"Of course not. She was 'married' to Ogbuide."

Chapter 10

"*Choo-shi, choo-shi, choo-shi.* What kind of goats are these? See, they are behaving like human beings. *Cho-oshi, cho-oshi.* Our ancestors protect us."

She threw the knife she was using in peeling the yam at the stubborn goats and missed. She hissed and went for her knife. She continued peeling the yam.

"You goats, go to sleep. It is late. You want to eat the peels, eh? You will not eat them. Do you hear? You will not eat them. Don't you know that there is famine, eh? Don't you see the way I am peeling the yam? I am going to use the peels for *ariba*. Do you hear? Who gives goats yam peels these days? Cassava is even expensive for goats these days.

"But must you be hungry from morning till night? Did you not find leaves to eat in the daytime? Our ancestors protect us!" Mgbeke exclaimed at the biggest one, a he-goat for that matter, for almost pushing her down with its head. She flung her knife at it and missed again:

"You wizard, what did you want to do with your head? You will not eat my yams today. Do you see my trouble? I don't have a goat and yet goats will not let me rest in this compound, goats will not let me drink water in this compound."

She began to shout:

"Those who have goats in this compound must look after them. I have chickens. They have turned in long ago. Come and take your goats-*o-o-o*."

One of the neighbors said, "The broken one, where did she go? Every day she comes home late. She is not the only fish-seller in this compound. I wonder when she cooks for her husband. The broken one, of course she does not cook for her husband anymore."

Then she said loudly for Mgbeke to hear, "The goats are mine, my sister."

"Then come and take them. Isn't it late?"

"I am coming, don't be angry with me. These goats are giving me a lot of trouble. How come they do not know the way home these days?"

Every night when everybody had gone to sleep, Mgbeke would stay up doing one thing or the other.

"I am notorious for cooking late in this compound. Besides cooking, I have this basket of fish to dry before I go to bed. But where is the foolish one? Where is my son? Isn't it time for him to come home, eh? As soon as he returns now, he will tell me that he went for choir practice, whatever that means, or that he went to play football. Football, today, choir practice tomorrow; one day, he is going to eat football and choir practice."

Mgbeke heard a shrill voice at a distance. Someone was hawking something and was shouting out what she was selling for anyone who cared to listen. She had finished peeling the yam and lit the fire. She was not sure whether she should eat the yams with palm oil or make pounded yam *foo-foo*. If she began to pound, the whole compound would hear and complain.

"Nonsense" she said. "I must pound the yam. I have very good dry fish to make a little rich soup. And besides, my son does not like chewing yam at night."

"These children… So, it is not time for them to go home? What are they selling?"

The shrill voices of the hawkers were getting louder and louder. It was now obvious to Mgbeke that the hawkers were aiming at her, for their voices could be heard clearly by now.

"You children, please leave. Go home. It is late. This is not the market place."

The children did not heed Mgbeke. They sang away:
"Bia zuru ni azu ego nioo."

Mgbeke shouted back at them:

"If they sent you to me this evening, tell them—those who sent you—that you did not see me."

"Bia zuru ni azu ego nioo" The children continued to sing.

"You children, I have done nothing to you. I am a poor fish-seller. I have to cook the evening meal, and I must rekindle this fire so as to dry my fish before I go to bed. It is this rain. It has been raining since yesterday and this morning it has not stopped. A child born today will never have a smile on her face."

"And see how damp and drab everything is. Look at this firewood. Was I not assured that it was dry and the best? Look at it now. And my fish will spoil. God forbid."

She poked the fire with a spear-like object, water dripping from her eyes and nose. She wiped her nose with the edge of her *wrappa*.

"You wait until I see that stupid child of mine. He goes to school in the morning, returns, eats and goes to play football or to choir practice."

"Bia zuru ni azu ego nioo."

"If these children think that I am going to leave this fire and go after them, they are mistaken. Let them stay there and shout. Imagine selling fish at the doorstep of one whose job is buying and selling fish. These children must be up to something. And where is Ekecha who should be here by now? What is keeping her at home? Is it that foolish husband of hers or one of the co-wives? I have told her to not bother about them."

"Bia zuru ni azu ego nioo."

"You children, bring your fish here."

"Who is that? Is that not my son's voice that I hear? The voice of his father? No, the voice is my son's. So that child of yesterday is turning into a man already? But what is he doing with fish? I have plenty of it here."

She went on attending to the fire. The yam was cooking.

"How much do you sell your fish?" asked Mgbeke's son.

Mgbeke held her breath, and suddenly it happened. The little girl who carried the basin that was supposed to contain the fish emptied the rubbish in the basin on the little boy, saying: "*Buru agbada nti ria maa.*" Her task performed, she fled with her basin and *utita*. Her companions had fled before her. Mgbeke's son burst into tears. Mgbeke rushed out of the kitchen.

"You foolish child; you good-for-nothing child. You rogue. What are you doing with fish? I have tons and tons of fish. I do nothing but buy and sell fish. Why do you want to buy fish? Thief. Sweet mouth. Look at his mouth, stop crying immediately."

She gave her son a big slap across his face and dragged him by his ear to the house.

"I thought you were strong. You are strong only at home where you beat up your sister. Foolish child, why are you crying? Why did you not pursue the child who sold mumps to you? You play football, therefore you can run. That child who did this to you is a mere girl; a girl, not a boy. My people, you are my witnesses. The children who have done this to my son, it will not be good for you. It will not be good for you in this world and in the world to come. My people, have you seen my trouble? Have you seen *ese* in all its ramifications? What have I done to deserve this? And what has my innocent foolish son done to deserve this?"

"Mgbeke, our Mgbeke, what is the matter?"

"Ekecha. Is that you? I don't blame you. You are the cause of this."

"What is the trouble? Who has annoyed you?" Mgbeke told the story.

"Ewoo, our Mgbeke, this is bad, very bad. In these hard times? Whose children have done this?"

Ekecha sympathized.

Neighbors gathered:

"Our Mgbeke, such a terrible curse, who annoyed you?"

"And where were you when those children were selling their mumps?"

"Don't worry about that. What happened?"

She narrated the story again.

"*Tufia, umu ojoo*. Where did they get mumps? Didn't their parents tell them that these things are no longer done in this way? Didn't they know that this is the time of the white people? I heard those children shouting:

'Come and buy fish, come and buy fish.' So, mumps were what they were selling? Mumps that is so contagious. Mgbeke, my sister, don't worry. Nothing will happen to your son. Don't curse the children. You may be cursing someone you are likely to take part in burying."

"Thank you, my sister," continued Ekecha. "It was partly my fault. If I had come on time, this could have been avoided. Mgbeke, please forgive me. And my friend's son, don't worry. You are not going to suffer from mumps. It is contagious, all right, but you don't get it that way, so the midwife in the Maternity Home told us."

"How do you get it?" asked Mgbeke, still in tears.

"When you drink water from the same cup used by someone suffering from it."

Mgbeke nodded and felt better. "But I must find out that child. Come here stupid one, you rogue who was asking for the price of fish, who gave you money to buy fish? Thief."

"It is enough," pleaded Ekecha.

"Didn't you recognize the children?"

The boy shook his head. He did not recognize them. It was getting dark. He did not even recognize the voice.

"You broken and foolish one, you went to the school to play football, isn't it? One day you will eat football. You will cook it in a pot and eat. I suffer to pay your school fees, buy books and uniform for you. I tell you to ask your father for school fees, you tell me he has no money. You have seen Nwanyiafor Okwosha with bags and bags of money."

"It is enough, Mgbeke. They all behave alike. Are you ready?"

"Ready?"

"Aren't you?"

"Don't you see the fish? I have to put them on the fire, at least for them to dry before cockcrow. The broken one over there has not eaten."

"Tomorrow then."

"What made you late?" Mgbeke asked.

"Let's not go into that now. It is a long story. Shall we go tomorrow?"

"Shall we go tomorrow? She mimicked. Then she said, "Tomorrow is Afo Ugbani."

"What about Orie?"

"She does not receive people on Orie."

"Eke then."

Mgbeke was silent.

"Tell me what made you late."

"Please don't rub it in. I am sorry."

"It is your daughter, not mine."

"I know."

"How is she now?"

"Much better." Ekecha sat more comfortably. "The moon is so bright," she said. "You can pick up a coin from the ground. I greet you, full moon—piece of yam that satisfies the whole universe."

They were silent again.

"Did she say much?"

"No. She talked slowly to herself. We did not understand what she said."

"And what did your husband say?"

"He said nothing."

"He said nothing?"

"You know he does not talk much."

"Beware of husbands who don't talk much." Ekecha smiled and said nothing.

"But he must have said something."

"Perhaps he had nothing to say."

"He had nothing to say. I can understand that. Keep quiet when you have nothing to say. That's the golden rule. Well, Eke will be the best day for me."

"Eke is all right for me too."

"Good. Tell me exactly what happened."

Ekecha began:

"My daughter and many other girls were swimming in the river. To be exact, there were six of them, all of the same age. They swam happily. Sometimes they dived and collected some white sand in the bottom of the river. Then my daughter dived and instead of a fist of sand, she picked a round smooth stone from the bottom of the river. The stone glittered like a precious stone. She showed the other children the stone. They all stopped swimming and examined the stone. Then an argument began. My daughter wanted to keep the stone, to show it to me when she got home. But the other five children wanted the stone thrown back into the river. My daughter bluntly refused, saying that she must show it to her mother.

"Unknown to the girls, a woman who had come to the river to wash her clothes was listening to them. The argument escalated to a quarrel. My daughter refused to let go the stone. The other girls tried to snatch it from her, but she held on to it. When it was obvious to my daughter that she was going to lose the stone, she swallowed it. And a fight ensued. The woman who was washing her clothes intervened. 'Don't fight, don't fight,' she pleaded. One of the girls told her own version of what happened. 'The stone belongs to all of us,' she concluded. 'And your mate has swallowed it?' asked the woman. 'Yes,' they chorused. 'Why did you swallow it?' 'It is mine, I found it,' said my daughter. 'She is lying.' 'She is lying. It belongs to all of us.' 'And they wanted me to throw it back into the river,' my daughter said. 'You did?' asked the woman. They fell silent. 'You cannot cut open your mate's stomach, can you?' They were silent. 'So, go home and–' 'They will kill us.' 'Who will kill you?' They fell silent. 'We want our stone.' 'My daughter was calm. She went for her *wrappa* and before her mates could stop her, she fled. They pursued her. She was a good runner. She ran. Luckily, I was home. She ran into my embrace. The children stopped pursuing her when they saw me. I asked them what was the matter, but they were silent. Then they went home. My daughter said nothing to me. She did not tell me that she had swallowed a stone.

"Seven days after, she was ill. She had very high fever. Her lips were blistered, she was unable to eat. I treated her for malaria. I gathered the plants, roots and leaves of pawpaw, lemon grass, *dogonyaro*, guava and lime. I cooked all these in a big pot as mother taught me. I gave her some to drink and bathed her with the hot water, but the fever did not go away. Then she began to talk to herself and I was alarmed. I did not understand what she said, but it was obvious that she was talking to someone who was listening to her. Then she began to see things that I could not see. She shouted that THEY had come to take her away, and that I should stop THEM from taking her away. At other times, she cried out and asked me to take a machete and cut THEM into pieces. She closed her eyes, and continued to say that she saw THEM.

"It was on the fifth day of her illness that the woman who was present at the river when she swallowed the stone came to me. She had meant to tell me immediately after it happened, but she had gone to Ose Anashi the day following the incident. "Did your daughter not tell you what happened?" she asked. "My daughter did not tell me," I said to her. She told me everything and how my daughter swallowed the stone. She advised me to see a medicine man. So, I went to Mgbada, Ona's father, and told him. He came to see my daughter. While he was prescribing the herbs and the sacrifices, my daughter began to shout. She called Mgbada's daughter, Idenu, by name and revealed that she was going back to the spirit world. She said that there was a big canoe full of children at Ose Ishibe. The children were travelling back to the spirit world. If nothing was done soon, Idenu would go in the canoe.

"Mgbada did not show much surprise at what my daughter said. He continued prescribing the herbs and when he finished, he said to her, "and when is your own canoe coming for you?" My daughter began to shout and protest. Mgbada asked calmly and clearly, "And where is it?" "Where is what?" my daughter asked angrily. "The stone. Your *iyi uwa*. Where is it?" My daughter began to cry again. "You did not swallow it?" asked Mgbada. "No. I did not." "What then did you swallow?" "Oh, that." "Yes, that." "The stone is not mine. It does not belong to me." "Is that right?" "I am speaking the truth." "Who does it belong to, then?" "My mates." "Those children who swam with you the day you got the stone?" She fell silent. "Go on, tell me. Let your mother know. I know you spoke the truth about my daughter, Idenu. I have taken precautions. She is not going to leave us for the spirit world. I have taken care of that." She said nothing. "The stone is still in your stomach?" "Yes." "You want it there because it is safe?" "Yes." "But it can harm you." "No." "It can." She shook her head. "We have to bring it out." She was silent. "So that your mates will live and not die." She said nothing. "Where then is yours?" She said nothing."

Mgbeke listened as if Ekecha was telling her a story from the spirit world. She wanted to know the intention of Ekecha's daughter. Why did she swallow the stone if it did not belong to her? Did she genuinely desire to stay with her earthly parents? Was she for or against her mates who were her spirit companions?

Ekecha went on with her story:

"So, Mgbada gave me some medicines. He warned me to watch my daughter. The following day, when my daughter emptied her bowels, the stone came out."

"It did?"

"Yes."

"And where is it?"

"With Mgbada."

"What was it like?"

"It was smooth and round and sparkled in the sun. Even at night, it sparkled"

"He has it now?"

"Yes."

"What is he going to do with it?"

"He will keep it. He had contacted the parents of the other children. Nothing will happen to them again."

"You said that there was a big canoe full of children at Ose Ishibe?"

"I said so, but it is no longer there." She said, "It has gone."

"Gone. It took a number of children though. This epidemic of measles."

"That's right. We were careful; our children did not suffer from measles."

"Yes, we took precautions. We did not expose our children to danger. My daughter was slightly affected, though. But thank God she is out of danger. The sacrifice is to appease the gods and our ancestors. As we had agreed, we shall perform the sacrifice on Eke."

Chapter 11

Mr. Sylvester, Ona's husband, arrived early at his father-in-law's house. Mgbada was crouched at the doorstep washing his face and hands. His son-in-law greeted him, "*Mazi*."

"My son, Chukwukere. Welcome, my son. There is a seat inside. I shall be with you shortly."

He soon joined Mr. Sylvester. "Welcome, my son. What about my daughter? I hope she is well. And our little son? Is he walking now?"

"We are all well, father; my son is walking," he said. He was a man of very few words. "Has mother gone to the market?"

"Market? No, she did not go to the market. She went to the mission. A new Father came to the parish, so she and other women had gone to welcome him and to present gifts to him."

"Of course, you are right. It was announced at mass last Sunday. In actual fact, I know the young man."

"The priest?" asked Mgbada.

"The priest. I know his parents very well. We come from the same place. His mother has seven of them."

"Seven of them?"

"Seven, all boys."

"And no girl?"

"And no girl."

"Lucky man," said Mgbada.

"He is indeed lucky; you can say that again. But…"

"I am listening."

"Five of them are in the priesthood."

"No!"

"And the two young ones are threatening to go, too."

"You don't mean it!"

"It is true."

"And what do the parents think? How do they feel about it?"

"Well…"

"Who is going to carry on?"

"You mean?"

"The family line. Who is going to hold the *ofo* of the ancestors?"

"Oh that."

"Yes, isn't it important to you?"

"Well, we are Christians, you know. We don't really bother ourselves with these things."

"I, too, I am a Christian. I go to church. I receive

the Holy Communion. But I still hold the *ofo* of my ancestors."

"Is it really possible to believe in the two?"

"Why not? I don't see anything wrong at all. I handle the two religions well. To me, none clashes with the other."

A long pause.

"How old are the parents?" asked Mgbada.

"Their father died last year. So, for their mother to be looked after properly, they sent her to a convent. And now the reverend sisters take good care of her."

"That's a neat way of doing it. And their ancestral home?"

"Their father was not the eldest son of his parents."

"I see. So, their uncle has taken over the ancestral home. Nobody should quarrel with that. But you say the younger brothers are also threatening to go into the priesthood. There must be something there."

Mr. Sylvester began to laugh.

"Have I amused you, my son-in-law?"

"You amuse me, father. Of course, there is something there."

"In the priesthood?"

"I guessed right. What is it?"

"Well, they are the priests of God. They are well taken care of. They receive free education, for instance."

"Free education?"

"The brothers go into the priesthood when they are very young. There they go to school. Everything is free."

"I did not know about this when I was growing up. Not that my father would have allowed me to go, I know that. But I wish that I had known. There were very bright boys in my village, brighter than I was, in fact, who dropped out of school because their parents could not pay their fees. But for my mother, I, too, could have been one of the dropouts. My mother tightened her loincloth, as we say, and made sure that I went as far as possible. So, you mean to tell me that the parents of these boys did not pay for their education?"

"Yes. They are poor, and when I say poor, I mean poor. Their father was a farmer; their mother also farmed around their house. When Christianity came to the village, they embraced it wholeheartedly. They had nothing to lose and a lot to gain. Their greatest assets were their boys. So, their mother just presented them one after the other to the white priests who came to the parish."

"That's wonderful. But don't you think that they can rebel? I mean, they can leave the priesthood at the slightest provocation."

"Or give a flimsy excuse, you mean?"

"Well, provocation or excuse, they are all one and the same to me. Then they leave the church and live normal lives again. That's what I mean."

"I understand you. The brothers are really godly. It is late in the day for them to do anything rash. They have gone a long way. If you talk of the younger ones, I can say that perhaps they have seen the advantage of it and want to go into it for what they can get and then quit."

"And nobody will blame them."

"If you say so, father."

"I say so. Sometimes I wonder why these people left their homes to come here and convert us to Christianity, without as much as understanding our own religions. Many times, I ask myself why they came. I think and think, but I don't arrive at any reasonable conclusion. So, what I am really driving at is this: if you go into the priesthood and sometime in your life wish to leave and do something else, you should be allowed to do so."

"That something else, father, is getting married?"

The two men roared with laughter.

"You have got my point, my son. You are a man. You know what I mean. That celibacy thing is nonsense. Don't you agree with me?"

"I agree with you, but they go into it with their eyes open. They know all the implications. Yet they elect to go. They are not forced, mind you."

"Force? The greatest force is poverty, my son. Poverty is bad. We pray to God and to our ancestors to make us wealthy, to keep poverty far away from us… I can hear my wife… it is, indeed, Akpe… Welcome, my wife. I did not expect you to return so early, welcome."

Akpe ignored him and greeted Ona's husband.

"Welcome, my son. I went to your house. Ona told me you were here. The young man is doing very well. He is taking his first steps. Babies, how fast they grow! Look at Ona of yesterday, a mother already. Take care of them. God's name be praised!"

"My wife, serve us kola nuts. I have been waiting for you to return. Ona's husband has been here for some time. Or don't you have kola nuts?"

"Joseph, did you think I was going to sleep in the mission?"

"Because I said you returned early? Don't mind me, my wife. It is just a matter of speaking. Serve us kola nuts if you have some."

Akpe said nothing. A gentle answer, they say, turns away wrath, though what was eating her up so early in the morning baffled her husband.

"My son, kola has come." He took it and he began:

> *My daughter's husband*
> *To your health*
> ***Ise***
> *You married my daughter*
> *Because she was*
> *Pleasing to your eyes*
> *May it be well for you*

May you prosper in our town
May good follow you
May bad things
Be far away from you.

May your wife, my daughter
Be fruitful and multiply
May your lovely son
Be followed by lovely sons
And sons and sons
Ise

My wife, to your health
You brought this kola nut
May it be well for you
May you continue to provide more
Ise

And to me
May it be well for me
May I continue to have the means
To provide for my children

And my wife
What are you waiting for?
I ask you our ancestors
What is keeping my wife

From bringing forth
More children?
Our ancestors,
May my wife have more
Children for me
Ise*.*

Akpe had left the room before her husband began the ritual of breaking the kola nut. Mr. Sylvester wondered at the things said and did not comment.

"My son-in-law, here is kola nut."

"*Mazi*." He took a lobe.

"My son, Chukwukere. *Akpe-oo, Akpe-oo* bring *kai kai*."

"It is too early, father."

"Too early? What will you use to wash down the kola? Water? No, we have good *kai kai. Akpe-oo*."

"Joseph, I am busy. You can see I am busy."

"Get us some *kai kai*. What are you busy about when our son is here? When Ona's husband is here? Or are you preparing breakfast for him? That's my wife. My son, my wife is preparing breakfast for us. You must wait and eat."

"Ona was preparing breakfast before I left her," Akpe grumbled.

"And so?"

Akpe brought the *kai kai* and two small glasses and

went back to the kitchen without saying a word. She had not, in fact, included Ona's husband in the meal she was preparing. Ona was cooking when she saw her. Now she had to include him. She wondered why her husband nearly always embarrassed her by inviting guests to meals when he had no idea what foods were available. She soon finished cooking and set the food on the table and excused herself.

The men ate and talked.

"I know you have come for something," said Mgbada when they finished eating.

"Come, let's sit more comfortably here," he said, getting up.

"Is it about your wife?"

"Yes."

"You have a problem?"

Mr. Sylvester nodded in agreement.

"What is the problem?"

"Ona is expecting another baby."

"May God Almighty be praised! And you say you have a problem? What do you mean?"

Silence.

"Go on, tell me. You have come to talk to me."

"The doctor said I should not touch her until our son is one year old."

Mgbada began to laugh.

"And you touched her," he laughed again. "And you are worried? And you say it is a problem?"

Mr. Sylvester was at a loss as to what to say.

"Shake my hand, my son. You are a man. A doctor told you not to touch your wife, my beautiful Ona, for one year? What kind of doctor is that? You mean these white doctors that come here once a month?"

"Yes, this one was a woman. But she said…"

"That's more understandable. Only a woman can say that kind of nonsense. Now, my daughter is pregnant?"

"Yes. The doctor said I should not touch her until our child is one year old," he repeated.

"I understand. How many months pregnant?"

"Three."

"Three already?"

"Yes. Three."

"What do you want to do?"

"I came to you for advice."

"You did well. What did the woman doctor say was wrong with my daughter?"

"She did not tell me."

"They are crazy people. Never mind. Listen to me; nothing will happen to your wife. I know a lot about these things. And my wife also knows that I know much about women and pregnancy. But she insisted that the doctors would take charge of Ona. I did not quarrel with her, but I kept my distance. Not anymore. I am going to take full charge now. Tell me, does Ona still breast-feed the child?"

"Yes."

"That is not right. She must stop breast-feeding immediately."

"Is that what you say?"

"Exactly. She must stop breast-feeding. Then send the baby to us. We shall take care of our grandson. Just as I say. Then you, my son, should try not to touch her. Do you hear me?"

"I hear you."

"You must not touch her until the pregnancy has advanced. Leave the rest to me. Nothing will happen to my daughter."

"Thank you. What about the hospital?"

"You mean the anti-natal?"

"Yes."

"Nothing stops her from attending. What they normally give them are iron and multivitamins."

"Does she eat well?"

"You know she is not one for large meals."

"I know she eats very little. Does she crave special foods?"

"Yes."

"Which ones?"

"Prawns and *iboro* which she eats raw."

"And what else?"

Mr. Sylvester thought.

"Doesn't she eat pounded yam with soup made with prawns?"

"She did during the first pregnancy. Not anymore. She eats plantains instead."

"Plantains?"

"Yes."

"Ripe or unripe?"

"Green ones roasted over the open fire."

"Really?"

"And she…"

"Go on…"

"Don't worry."

"Go on, say it all."

"She sometimes talks to herself."

Long pause.

"Do you mean in her dream?"

"No, in broad daylight."

"What does she say?"

"I don't understand what she says. She just talks. Sometimes it appears to me that she is not aware of what she is doing or saying."

"You are a good son-in-law. You have done well to come to me. Ask Ona to come and see me. I want to talk to her. As for her pregnancy, she will be all right. I am going to give her specially prepared herbs."

"Thank you, father."

"Thank you, my son, go well, my son."

The next morning, quite early, Mgbada travelled to Ila to consult a medicine man and a diviner about his daughter, Ona.

Chapter 12

"Ona, my daughter, welcome. Your husband told you I wanted to see you?"

"Yes, father. I had wanted to see you before my husband gave me the message."

"Is that so?"

"Yes, father."

"What did you want to tell me? Is it Idenu?"

"Yes, father."

"I have taken care of everything."

"Yes, father, but…"

"Go on."

"There are other things."

"Tell me."

"I saw them in my dream."

"Go ahead."

"It seems as if Idenu's *iyi uwa* is buried in a particular fish."

"Fish?"

"Yes. And I would like her to stop eating that kind of fish."

"What fish?"

"*Asa*."

"*Asa*?"

"Yes."

"Unbelievable. The greatest of all fishes?"

"Yes. I say so because each time I see *asa* I see Idenu's face."

"How?"

"I see her face this minute, another minute I see *asa* in place of her face."

"That is strange. I have done all I was told to do. I can say that she is out of danger. She will stay with us."

"She must not eat *asa* fish."

"Is that what you said?"

"Yes, father."

"Good, I shall tell your mother and your two grandmothers."

They fell silent. A song was heard from afar. Children of the compound were singing:

"*Nde muo jere omerife eriwo nni, iwe n'e we wo*"

Father and daughter burst into laughter.

Mgbada called: "Come, my children, come and sing your song for us."

The children came; there were six of them, all

young boys. They sang the song again, and when they finished, Mgbada said:

"But this is not the time to sing this song, my children."

The children said nothing.

Mgbada went on:

"The song is sung during the new yam festival."

"We know."

"Good. If you know, why sing it now?"

"We are singing it for Ona."

"For Ona?"

"Yes," chorused the children.

Ona said nothing.

"Why are you singing it for Ona?"

"They asked us to sing the song for her," replied one of the children.

"Your mates?"

"Yes."

"In the spirit world?"

They said nothing.

Ona said nothing.

"*Nde muo jere omerife eriwo nni, iwe n'e we wo,*" they sang.

"You are hungry, then?"

"We are hungry," the children said.

"My wife has not returned from the market. I have nothing for you in the house."

"We are going. *Nde muo jere omerife eriwo nni…*"

"Wait," Ona said. "You want food?"

"We want food."

"Who sent you?"

"Our mates," some said.

"Ogbuide," others said.

"To me?"

They fell silent.

"Tell me, did she send you to me?"

They said nothing.

"If she or your mates sent you to me, come to my house. This is not my house."

"This is your father's house."

"Correct."

"It is your home. Here is your home. Your umbilical cord was buried here."

"But I am married."

"We know. You must return to your father's house. *Nde muo jere…*"

"What kind of children are these?"

"Did you recognize any of them?"

"Not one. They are not from this village. I can assure you."

"They will come to me."

"You think so?"

"I know; they will come. You sent for me, father?"

"Yes, are you well?"

"I am well, father."

"And your son?"

"He is well."

"Your husband has gone home."

"Yes, father."

Mgbada cleared his throat and said: "Your husband came to me before he travelled."

"Yes, father," Ona detected anxiety in his voice. She waited. Mgbada cleared his throat again. "Can I get you some water?"

He hesitated, and said yes. Ona went into the room and brought some water for her father to drink. He drank a little and put down the glass.

"Your husband came to me," Mgbada said in an urgent voice. "Tell me, do you have peculiar dreams?"

"Yes, father."

"You do?"

"Yes, father."

"Tell me some of your dreams."

Ona told her father the dreams she dreamt often of her journeys to the bottom of the Lake where she mingled with fishes with the heads of humans; where the Woman of the Lake lived with the creatures of the water; where there was no darkness but light; and where everyone was contented.

"You mingled with our mother?"

"Yes."

"What did she say to you?"

"Nothing."

"Did she give you anything to eat?"

"No."

"Tell me more."

"When I wake up, I don't see her again."

"And you want to see her?"

"I love to see her. I have a sense of well-being when I dream my dreams."

"Your husband is worried about the dreams. Have you ever told him your dreams?"

"No."

"You should tell him when you dream strange dreams."

"All right."

"And do you talk to yourself sometimes?"

"I don't know father."

"Your husband said that you sometimes talk to yourself. He said that you sometimes see visions."

Ona was silent.

"We have to find out what is wrong with you."

"There is nothing wrong with me, father."

Mgbada was silent.

"You gave us a lot of trouble when you were a child."

"What kind of trouble?"

"You were in the habit of disappearing at will."

"Really, why was I disappearing?"

He did not answer. He said, "We think that Ogbuide is responsible. We have to consult medicine men and diviners. We have to put a stop to your strange ways so that you can be worthy of your good husband."

"I hear you, father."

"And you are expecting another baby?"

"Yes father."

"You are going to have your baby without difficulty."

"Yes father."

"Now go home and be a good wife to your husband."

"Yes father."

When Ona left, Mgbada summoned Akpe, Mama Theresa and Nwafor. He told them what Mr. Sylvester told him. The women were upset.

"Our people have told our in-law about Ona's peculiarities," said Nwafor.

"No, my mother. Ona's husband came to me. We all know Ona's problems. We know that Ona is not normal. It is our duty to make her normal so that she can be worthy of her good husband, the husband that was given to her on a platter of gold, so we have to put heads together. I need your support. Ona did not seem to know much about her problems. We must be wary of enemies. So, we must keep Ona's problems close to the family. We do not want a scandal of any kind. We all must work together to save Ona's marriage."

"We must save Ona's marriage," the women agreed.

"We must through prayer," said Akpe.

"Amen," said Mama Theresa.

"Seek and you shall find," said Akpe.

"Knock and it shall be opened unto you," said Mama Theresa.

"We shall pray to God. We shall also consult the medicine men and women of note. Akpe and mother, you pray, while my mother and I travel to Ila to seek help."

Akpe began to weep softly.

"Why are you weeping?" asked her mother. "My God is alive. The God I worship night and day will do what I ask Him to do for me. Wipe your tears. Mary, Mother of Jesus, is alive. We shall not be shamed."

"People will talk. People will say that my daughter is mad," wept Akpe.

"Have faith, my wife. Pray to God and I shall seek help from diviners."

"People will say that there is insanity in our family," Akpe continued weeping.

"You must stop that nonsense, Maria," scolded Mama Theresa. "Don't you hear your husband? Have faith in God." Mama Theresa began to count her chaplet.

Akpe brought out hers, too, and began to pray. "Our good fortune did not last long," Akpe wept. "I had thought that all was well with my daughter when she married. I now know that all was not well."

"All will be well, my daughter," consoled Mama Theresa.

Mgbada returned from his journey and assembled the women again.

"There is nothing we can do," he announced.

There was silence.

Mgbada went on: "We cannot fight against our Mother."

"Our Mother?"

"Uhamiri?"

Silence.

"Ogbuide?"

"Eze nwanyi?"

"Eze miri?"

"She answers to these names," continued Mgbada. "She is one and the same spirit. Her spirit troubles our daughter. We cannot fight her. The *dibia* was unequivocal. Ona has been called. Ona has been chosen. Ona must heed the call. Ona has no choice."

"And if she did not heed the call?"

"Shhh. Don't say it aloud; the spirits may hear you. Are you crazy?" responded Mama Theresa.

"Mother, but I thought…"

"Don't think anything. We have no choice in the matter. Didn't we all know this long before now? So, let us be realistic about it. We have to protect the good name of the family."

"And the church cannot do anything for Ona?"

"You did try the convent. Father Millet did pray for her, but the ailment persisted," replied Mama Theresa.

"She can go into the nunnery," suggested Akpe.

"Nunnery?" Mama Theresa asked and appealed to Nwafor and Mgbada to put in a word. "I prefer the nunnery to this Ogbuide thing. My whole being revolts against it."

There was silence.

Then Mgbada began: "I am happy that you suggested the nunnery because you have now accepted that there is indeed something seriously wrong with our Ona. So we are, in fact, getting somewhere. But you ignore one serious point. The nunnery, according to my understanding, is not a dumping ground. You have to be called by God to serve. You have to be married to Christ. Our Ona, as you know, does not care about the church. She always needed a cane to make her go to mass when she was a child. And she hated school where she could have learnt catechism."

"My son-in-law has spoken well. We have to move forward. What did the *dibia* say we must do, now that we have accepted that Ona has been chosen by the woman of the Lake as her priestess? That's where we must direct our energy. My daughter, I am a Christian, too. It is too late in the day to think of the nunnery. Your husband has said that the nunnery is not a dumping ground. If Ona were not my granddaughter, I would have concluded that she was mad. As mad as Eziti. So, make no mistake about it. We have to turn to another direction. We have, in fact, turned to another direction for help. So, listen to your husband. Make it easier for him. You can see that he is handling the case admirably. He has gone to Ila and back. Let us listen to him. Over to you, my son-in-law."

"Thank you, my mother-in-law. My wife, you have heard your mother say 'The family's reputation is at stake. We shall do everything in our power to save our daughter and her marriage.' We shall be objective. I don't say don't pray. I say go on and pray, while we try what the *dibia* I consulted in *Ila* prescribed."

"According to what the *dibia* told me, we have to let Ona be. Ona must be herself. We must not hinder her in any way. She likes water, for instance we must allow her to swim in the Lake, in the river or in the stream. We must encourage her to swim, to do the things she loves doing. She is merely doing what the deity asks her to do. She is obeying orders from a force greater than all of us."

"And her marriage?" asked Akpe. "If we let her do all these, then she would not be able to be her husband's wife."

"You are right, my wife. The question is this: should we let her husband know about her calling now? My wife has a point there."

Nobody spoke.

"I don't know how I am going to take the news when I am told that my wife is the chosen priestess of a deity." he went on. Nobody spoke. He continued:

"Our son-in-law is already worried. He came to me. He told me about Ona's problems. Must we tell him he shares his wife with a deity?"

"And save the marriage?" said Akpe.

"This is the point I was trying to stress."

"We have a problem here." said Nwafor.

"Ona is pregnant." said Mama Theresa.

"Yes."

"Let's wait until she has the baby. You never can tell. Ogbuide might reject her."

There was silence.

"Ogbuide might reject her," thought Mgbada.

"Is it possible?" asked Nwafor.

"It has happened before," said Mama Theresa.

"It happened when our forefathers ate with both hands."

"It may happen again, you never can tell, "Mama Theresa said to Mgbada.

"So, we wait until Ona's baby is born?"

"Yes," said everybody.

Ona had two more babies; the last one was named Veronica after Mr. Sylvester's mother. She appeared normal to everybody. She began to take her responsibility as a wife and mother more seriously. She was no longer reminded, for instance, by her husband to buy foodstuffs on Nkwo because it was cheaper for her to do so. Her husband did not have to struggle with her before he made love to her. She accepted it as her duty to surrender herself to him whenever he wanted her to do so. Sex was something that was strange, even alien, to her. Why did men make so much fuss about it? What was it that men enjoyed? It was dirty, as far as she was concerned. What with the slimy stuff between her legs when it was all over. If she had her way, she would have none of it.

Did she like her husband? She did not give a thought to it. Did it really matter whether she liked him or not? Her parents and grandmothers liked him and told her that he was a good man. Who was she to contradict these important people in her life? She was satisfied that she had done what was expected of her. She had given her husband three children in nearly five and a half years. That was a record. What baffled her was the fuss made by everyone related to her about her children.

Did she really care whether she had a child or not? Thinking seriously about it, she did not care one way or the other for her children. Did she not possess the instincts of a mother? Why was she not excited like everyone else about her children, such beautiful children?

Her husband. He must be a very patient man to

put up with her and her peculiarities. She remembered a night she woke up crying. Her husband had woken her and asked her gently what was wrong. She had gone on crying. He had wiped her tears and had brought her favorite fish, *iboro*. She had stopped crying instantly and began to eat the fish. It was not in season then, where did her husband get it? She thought that it was that night that she conceived her third child, and it was also that night, she thought, that she nearly experienced an orgasm. Perhaps, she thought, it was time for her to be a little bit closer to her husband. He was the only male, apart from her father, who was close to her. She did not think much about her brothers. They were rather distant. She had to make an effort to be good to this man who was her husband. But when she tried, she failed woefully. There was something beyond her, some force that prevented this closeness. Try as she could, it was impossible. She had thought it over so much that she decided to take her father into confidence. Her father had told her not to worry so long as she was happy and performed her wifely duties. It bothered her, nonetheless, in spite of her father's assurances.

But why did she not confide in her mother or her two grandmothers? They were in a better position to help her, being women. Try as she could, it was not easy for her. No, she must do something about her relationship with her husband. She must be nice to him.

Perhaps she could try and initiate the lovemaking once in a while. She tried this one night and it worked. She saw the effect it had on her husband. He left home in the morning feeling high. He had returned from the market bringing her gifts, *george*, head-tie, biscuits, and sweets. So, that was it? That was the secret? She had to do it more often then. After what passed for a long period, she tried the intimacy again. It worked, but when it was over and her husband was snoring with contentment, Ona was tossing in bed. She could not sleep.

It was at cockcrow that she thought she eventually slept, but not for long, for she saw a naked woman standing in front of her. She had very long hair dripping with water. She had on coral and agate beads on her neck and wrists. Her eyes were sharp and penetrating, they were piercing her body.

"Who are you?" Ona found her voice.

Silence.

"Who are you?" she repeated.

"I say, who are you?"

The woman disappeared.

"What is the matter?" asked her husband.

Ona shook herself awake; cold sweat dripping down her face.

"What is the matter?" Mr. Sylvester asked again.

"I saw a woman."

"A woman?"

"A naked woman."

"Where is she?"

"She has disappeared. I don't see her anymore."

"It is a dream. Go to sleep. You can see the door is locked."

"I saw her..."

"Lie down; come closer; go to sleep." He touched her, but she protested vehemently. "Why?" Mr. Sylvester asked in surprise and got up. When he looked at the clock, he saw that it was six in the morning. He was going to a faraway market. He went to the bathroom, had his bath quickly and prepared to leave. "I am ready, Ona, are you awake? Go back to sleep. You were dreaming. Buy yourself some biscuits and sweets." He gave her some money which she took without saying thank you.

He was gone before Ona could recollect herself. She sat on the bed with her hand on her chin and wondered about what she saw. It was no dream at all, she told herself a dozen times. "I saw this woman with my own naked eyes," she said. It was time to see her father and confide in him. Her husband had told her many times that she spoke in her sleep. She did not recollect what she said. So, she denied that she ever spoke while she slept. Now it was true. Her father should have an answer. She must go to him.

"My daughter is coming to see me today," Mgbada told Akpe when she was getting ready to go to the church for angelus.

"Joseph, I know that you are a seer, but you are not going to stop me from going to the mission."

"Father, *mazi*."

"Who is that?" Akpe asked from within.

"Come out and see who it is," said Mgbada.

"Mother, it is me."

"Ona."

"Mm."

"Ona."

"Mm."

"You must have arranged this with your daughter,"

Mgbada laughed. What his wife did not understand was that he was a great *dibia*. Was it, indeed, a matter of understanding? No. It was a matter of a prophet being without honor in his own house.

Ona's people said it in this way: "The beauty of a woman is only appreciated by outsiders."

"Are you going to the mission?" Ona asked her mother who was still inside the room.

"Yes, right away. Why not come in?"

"I shall see you here, mother. I have Veronica on my back."

Akpe came out. "Welcome, my daughter. We have not seen you for quite some time now." She turned to the child on Ona's back: "Veronica, how are you? Stay with your father, I am coming back soon."

She was gone.

"She has gone?" said Mgbada in disgust. "I am glad my mother is not as fanatical about her religion as my wife. She should have stayed back. Does she know why you are here? She knows that you never visit unless there is something you want to talk about. There is tomorrow and next tomorrow. There are many more tomorrows, why doesn't she stay today and be with you?"

"Father, she cannot help herself."

"I can see that. Welcome, my daughter. You are looking well. How are your husband and children? Veronica, welcome. Bring her down so I can take a closer look at her. How you have grown? How many months is she now?"

"Ten months."

"Is she standing?"

"She is walking, father."

"Walking at ten months. Your namesake must have been a smart and strong woman. So, you must take after her." Mgbada said. "Your mother is not in to bring kola for us."

"You know I don't eat kola."

"What do you really eat, my daughter?"

"You know, father."

"Prawns, *iboro* and all that. These are no foods."

"Father has come again," Ona began to laugh.

"You say your husband is well?"

"He is well. He left early this morning for the market at Orie Omuma."

"Ahaa, today is Orie Omuma; they have plenty of goats and sheep in that market. So, your husband went there?"

"Yes, he sells his medicines there."

"That's good. I hope you are living in peace."

"We are living in peace, father."

"You have come to see me."

"Yes, father. My dreams."

"Tell me."

Ona told her father her dreams. When she finished, her father said:

"These are good dreams, my daughter. When next you dream such dreams, tell your husband."

"Mm?"

"Yes, tell your husband."

"I cannot tell him."

"Why?"

Silence.

"I say tell him. Let us hear what he would say, then come and tell me what his reactions are."

"You think that I should?"

"Why not? You are in a better position to tell him. You see he is not from our town. He is a stranger. He may have something fresh and important to say. I think that you should tell him, not me, not your mother or your grandmothers."

"I have heard you, father."

"Good. Try to be closer to him. I know that it is difficult you being much younger than he, and shy. I can see far, my daughter. If you play your card well, your husband might go along with you. You have a great future. Our business is to guide you, but we cannot influence what will happen. What is written is written. I wish I could do something about it. I cannot. I have thought about you very seriously. I knew you would come today, and I knew why you came before you told me. You are going to shoulder great responsibilities in future. I had wished it did not fall on you to perform such an arduous task. But who are we to choose? You have been called and you have to obey. Failure to heed the call could mean disability or even death."

Silence.

"Father, you talk in parables. I no longer understand you."

"That's your mother."

"Ona, so you are still here. Stay and eat. I bought fresh fish and your favorite prawns. These ones are from Uhamiri, not from Oruru or Urashi."

She waited and when her mother finished cooking, she ate, but not with relish. She did not quite understand what her father said to her. He said she was called, called by whom? He said she was going to be great and that she had a great future. What did all these mean? She wanted to be just herself, Ona. She was beginning to feel happy in her marriage. Why didn't they leave her alone, just to be herself, swim in the Lake, fish and dance when necessary, with her age-grade? She did not understand all the fuss.

Everybody was trying to make her larger than she really was. The children had come to her saying that they had a message from the Goddess of the Lake. When she asked them to give her the message, they said that they had forgotten. She could not understand it. She had persuaded them to stay and eat. They had agreed to stay, but when she finished cooking, they refused to eat the food. She was not happy with them. She threatened to beat them up if they refused to give her the message. When she went into her room, the children, six in all, had run away except one of them who had a bad leg.

"I did not want to run away," he said to her. "The message is this," he went on, "you must go back to your father's home. This place is not your home. This is the message. I am going." And he was gone.

Chapter 13

It was Mr. Sylvester's habit to leave his young wife and children sleeping while he got ready to go to the market. That morning he got up reluctantly, sleep was still in his eyes, he had not had a good sleep; his children cried a lot at night and Ona had problems calming them. Mr. Sylvester left this to Ona for he was not good at putting the children to sleep when they cried. He went to the bathroom, had his bath slowly, dried himself with a towel, tied the towel round his waist and entered the room. Ona was standing in front of him. This was unusual.

Ona normally would be sleeping, and when he got ready to go, he'd wake her up and then leave. "Ona," he called.

She motioned him to sit down. He sat down. Ona's eyes were closed. She was standing. She was motionless, like a statue.

"Listen to me," she said in a loud, clear voice, "listen to my dream. I dreamt. I was swimming in the Lake. Different kinds of fishes were swimming with me. When they dived, I dived. They were surprised because I swam better than they did. There was a very huge one. It was as big as a house. Its fins were like wings. The fins had black, blue and yellow spots. They were beautiful to behold. This big fish was the leader of all the fishes. Wherever it swam to, the others followed it, and I followed. We swam to the bottom of the Lake. We saw the white sand, sparkling like silver. The leader stopped and we all stopped. I heard three knocks from nowhere. Then three more knocks in acknowledgement of the first three. Then a big golden gate began to open slowly. As it opened, we saw nothing but space, space upon space. We followed the leader.

"This time I was not sure whether we were swimming, floating or flying. All I knew was that we were moving, moving and moving. Then we saw another body of water. It was still like the color of the Lake. It was fresh and clear and clean. There were thousands and thousands of different kinds of fishes. They made way for us. Some very big ones stood guard while we passed.

"I wondered. But I was not afraid. I enjoyed the journey, if indeed it would be called a journey. All that was in my mind was to get to the end of this journey. We swam, or floated or flew or walked. Then again, we saw a huge golden gate. This one was bigger and more beautiful than the first one. No knock was heard this time. The gate opened and we all went in. Then, suddenly I was alone. I looked to the right and to the left. I looked behind me and in front of me, and I saw nobody. But I was not afraid. I must see the end of this journey, I said to myself.

"I was not tired. I was not wet. I did not feel my own weight. This kind of weightlessness frightened me only for a while, for I soon got used to it. *Well*, I asked myself, *is this the end of the journey?*

"It is not the end of the journey," said a voice. "You wait and see." I was not afraid so I said to the voice, "I don't have to wait till eternity to come to the end of this journey." The voice replied, "This is not the end of the journey. It is only the beginning."

"It was then that I became afraid. I tried to wake up from my sleep but I could not. Yes, I knew I was dreaming. I was very much aware that it was only a dream and that I would wake up and be my normal self again."

Ona stopped abruptly. Mr. Sylvester was glued to the seat, his towel around the waist. The children were still sleeping. The cock had crowed the second time. Mr. Sylvester normally left at the second crow of the cock. He was blown away by his wife's account of her dream. It seemed to him as if a force glued him onto his seat.

Ona continued:

"Then there was a mild commotion—the kind that signaled the arrival of a guest of honor, or a very important person. Then two little teenage girls appeared. They were like Siamese twins. They were very fair, with long plaited hair. They wore coral beads around their necks and wrists. They were barefoot. They walked towards me. Again, I was not afraid. They walked in measured steps. They carried identical bowls in their hands. They turned their backs on me. Then they knelt down; raised the bowl up as in supplication.

"Then I heard some drumming. At first it was slow, but it became faster. As it became faster, it became louder as well. Then to my horror, snakes of all colors and sizes began to crawl out. I froze. They crawled past me. Thank God.

"Then a terrific flash cut the air. It nearly blinded me. Another flash, and yet another. It illuminated the place; it was like daylight. Daylight under the water. But I saw nothing, only a great expanse of space. There was no cloud and there was no water. I saw all this in seconds.

"Then came thunder. It dawned on me that the flash was lightning, but lightning of a different kind of intensity. I closed my eyes. But even as my eyes remained closed, I could see all around me. Yet, I saw nothing. When it was all over, a sudden calm descended on me. Then I saw a shadow. I was not sure whether it was my own shadow or not. It was tall, so it could not be mine. The shadow walked majestically out of nowhere towards me. I stood petrified. The shadow was elegant and stately. There was a kind of aura around it. There was evidence that it was not alone. I looked and I saw the two Siamese twins. They still raised the bowls high. They were kneeling now.

"As it approached, it took another form. It was no longer a shadow but a woman. Yes, a woman. She was naked except for the hundreds of strings of coral beads around her waist. She had two strings of coral beads on both wrists, and hundreds around her neck. Down to her navel, water was dripping from her wet hair, yet she was not wet. She held a gold staff of office in her right hand.

"I stared at her. I looked into her eyes that were sharp and penetrating. They were sparkling like diamonds. The Siamese twins got up and walked towards her. At her feet they stopped and knelt down. She did not notice them. When I looked again, they had disappeared.

"Then she said, 'It has taken you a very long time to come.' She smiled and touched my right shoulder with her staff. 'Welcome to my abode,' she said. She continued, 'I have waited for a long time for you to be my priestess. I have chosen you. I want you but I don't want to force you nor hurry you. Don't wait too long. Give this message to the man who lives with you: Tell him you belong to me. Tell him to…' I woke up. I heard you enter the room. What kind of dream is this?"

Mr. Sylvester said nothing. He put on his clothes; combed his hair. One of the children began to cry. Ona picked him up, put him on her back, tied him securely with a cloth and rocked him.

"You have not said anything," Ona said. She continued, "You are going to sell all your goods at the market today."

Mr. Sylvester said nothing. What was going on in his mind? What was he going to do about his family? Did he in fact marry a spirit? Ona must be a spirit to be able to communicate with those in the spirit world. She repeated, "You are going to sell all your goods at the market today."

Was this a prophesy? The problem was beyond him. Dream. What a dream! A woman underneath the water. All fantasy. And yet and yet…

"Are you not going to the market?"

Mr. Sylvester stared at his wife.

"What are you waiting for?"

Mr. Sylvester thought: "She is still in the spirit world. She is dreaming her dreams. She is still…"

"You have been standing there for a while now, are you trying to remember something?"

Mr. Sylvester said to himself, "I am a man. Ona is my wife. I am her husband. There is no problem that I cannot solve. This is not the first time. When I return from the market, I shall see her father and talk things over with him. Ona is a mere child. A woman at the bottom of the Lake? A kind of palace underneath the water? It is a dream; a very imaginative one, indeed."

Then he said to his wife, "I am late already, but I must go now. Take care of the children. Visit your mother if you like. And the dr…" he stopped.

Mr. Sylvester could not concentrate in the market. He sold his medicines, bought more from others and sold them too. But rather than go home, he went to see Ona's father.

Mgbada was sitting in his *obi* as usual. He had just dismissed a woman and her daughter who came to consult him. They had brought him some gifts of kola nuts, yams and a chicken, and he was pleased.

Then his son-in-law arrived and greeted him: "*Mazi*."

"My son, Chukwukere. You are rather early today. Did you sell anything?"

"Market is bad. But why should we complain? Everything is in the hands of God. The day I make good sales, I thank God; the day I don't make good sales, I thank God. We are mere mortals in the sight of the Almighty God. We must continue to thank him for being born and for breathing the air He gave us in abundance."

"Good talk, my daughter's husband. Whoever does

not acknowledge the power of the Almighty God is a fool. Who are we to question His actions? He is beyond comprehension. Welcome, my son. Have something to cool you."

"Don't worry, *mazi*," He got up to go. "I thought I should come and see you. I am traveling tomorrow morning, and am not sure when I shall return."

"You did well, my son-in-law. You are considerate. Your wife and the children, are they well?"

Mr. Sylvester sat down again before he replied that they were well.

"You don't sound convincing."

"They are well. Ona told me something this morning."

"I am listening to you."

"Rather strange."

"Go ahead, tell me."

"What we can call seeing a vision."

"I understand you. She dreamt?"

"Exactly, she dreamt and she told me her dream."

"And what she told you came to pass?"

"Yes, but how did you know?"

"I am her father. My father was a medicine man. I am a medicine man, though I have watered down my own power and skill with Christianity and book knowledge."

"She was born with this gift then?"

"Gift, that's it, my son-in-law. It is a gift, a rare gift. She was born with it. I am glad that you see it that way."

"Some people could misunderstand it, and think that it is…" he stopped.

"Madness. Out with it, my son."

"Madness, people of lesser understanding would think that way. I don't think that it is madness. I have little understanding. I know…" he trailed off. "We have to harness this gift," he said slowly.

"You are right, my son. How do we go about it? You are a Catholic; so am I. The church frowns on such things."

"It has nothing to do with the church," said Mr. Sylvester. "The Bible says give unto Caesar what is Caesar's and to God what is God's."

"My wife should hear this."

"We had our own religion before the missionaries came."

"I agree with you, my son-in-law."

"We have to take care of Ona properly. This morning she told me something. It happened as she said it. Didn't a woman and her daughter come to you today?"

"They left before you arrived. I told them what to do."

"What did you tell them?"

"I prescribed some sacrifices for them. The church does not know much about sacrifices, and if it does it does not want us to make use of them. There is something in our religion or tradition or custom, call it what you will;

we call *ese*. Your people call it *uke*, others, *ogba n'uke*. It visits everybody born of a woman. It is evil. It is beyond understanding. When it visits you, you have to make sacrifices in order to ward it off. *Ese* visited the woman's child so I prescribed a form of sacrifice, not medicine."

"I understand."

They talked for a little while, then Mr. Sylvester said, "I have to go home now, father."

"Already? I thought you wanted to see me about something."

Mr. Sylvester fell silent.

"Tell me, my son. I am a medicine man, you know. You have something on your mind. I detected that immediately when you arrived. You were so philosophical. What is it? Tell your father-in-law. Maybe he can be of help."

"I have something on my mind."

"I know. Ona?"

"Ona."

"Get it off your chest."

He fell silent.

"Take me into confidence as you did before."

"All right I must go on, it is getting late. I want to think it over. I don't want to rush things. I want to know more about Ona so that I can understand more. Ona is a rare child, a strange child, and…"

"Don't worry. You can tell me when you are ready to do so."

Chapter 14

Mgbeke and Ekecha were in their light canoe on the Lake. They were going to buy fish for sale when they saw Ojoru, the ferrywoman.

"Our Ojoru," began Mgbeke, "so you come this far?"

"Is that you, Mgbeke?"

"Yes, it is Mgbeke and her friend, Ekecha."

"Two friends, are you going to buy fish?" asked Ojoru.

"And you are ferrying people across the Lake. *Onye na nke ya no na ugbo oyibo.*"

"That's what it is. We have to live and living means struggling. I wonder when it would all end."

"Don't say that, our Ojoru," said the two women.

"Go well, my sisters. May the Woman of the Lake break kola nuts for you today."

"Thank you. She will do the same for you."

"You were telling me about your daughter. How is she?" Mgbeke asked Ekecha.

"Oh, Miss. She is fine."

"Miss? You call her Miss?" asked Mgbeke.

"Everybody calls her that."

"Who is everybody, your children?"

"Yes, my children, and the pupils she was teaching before she went to the convent at Ose Akwa."

"And so, you too must forget her name and call her Miss? What is Miss?"

"I don't know. We are ignorant. We did not go to school."

"Nothing will make me call my daughter Miss. I call her by her name. I make her cook when she returns home during the holidays. She will not sit at home and expect me to return from the market and cook for her. Our gods and goddesses forbid. She tried it with me and she starved. I refused to cook for her. Education should teach them to respect their parents, not to look down on them. I suffer to pay her school fees. Miss indeed!"

"You pay too?" added Ekecha. "I paid her school fees when her father refused to pay because he wanted to marry another wife. I begged him afterwards to help me. He refused, saying that my daughter should marry. I said to him, 'Do husbands drop from heaven? Let her continue to acquire some education so as to improve herself; a husband would come.' But he would hear none of it. That's why I am suffering, trying to make ends meet. One day, my daughter will find a husband. And when she does, her father will sit majestically in his *obi* to welcome his in-laws and to boast about his daughter. Very unfair. Nobody will remember me on that day."

"Then you don't know me. You wait until a good husband comes. I am clear in my mind what I am going to do. The clothes I am going to wear are right in the bottom of my box. If I don't buy a string of aka beads before then, I am going to borrow one from Mama Nwafor, Mgbada's mother. You will not recognize me on that day. I am going to show everybody that I am the mother of the bride. You remember how Mama Nwafor dressed the day Akpe got married? That's the way I am going to dress. Except that I am not going to wear coral beads. Everybody will know at once that I had borrowed them. But I know that before I die, I must buy a string of coral beads."

"We were talking about Ona," Ekecha reminded her friend.

"I am coming to that, my friend. What's happening today? Why are there no fishermen on the Lake? We are getting to the Urashi River."

"I saw two fishermen early this morning when I was going to Obana," said Ekecha.

"Me too. I saw Okonyia and Eneberi with their nets this morning. Where are they?"

"Are we late?"

"Late? On Eke? No. We are not."

"Because Okonyia and Eneberi are fond of selling their fish at Ngo," said Ekecha.

"Greedy people."

"They say we cheat them."

"They cannot be fishermen, as well as fish-sellers. Do we force them to sell to us?"

"Somehow Eneberi knew, I don't know from whom, what profit we made on the *asa* and *atuma* we bought from him a long time ago."

"The ones that Ona and the Father's cook bought?"

"Yes."

"That's market. But that was a long time ago. Sometimes you gain, other times you lose; that's market."

"Let's stop over there and rest." She indicated where she meant with her paddle. "The sun is getting stronger and stronger."

They paddled their canoe further left and went ashore where a big tree provided a shade. It was better for them to wait there for the fishermen than paddle on and on. Mgbeke and Ekecha washed their faces and evoked the Goddess of the Lake.

"How fresh the water is!"

"May she be praised!"

"Our Mother is supreme."

"Who can question that?"

"Year in, year out, she is the same."

"The hairy woman."

"The elegant spirit."

"Bring fishermen to us."

"Fishermen who have caught fishes."

"We are your children, and we are women like you."

"We sell fish caught in your water."

"Isn't she great?" said Mgbeke at last.

Nothing happened.

"You were talking about Ona, what happened to her?" asked Ekecha.

"Ona, may she be blessed! We say she is mad."

"So, we say, isn't she mad?"

"I don't know any more. I now hear that she gets on very well with her husband."

"True."

"Very true. That's why I say that a child of a great woman or man, no matter what happens, no matter how badly she behaves, or whatever illness possesses her, is usually useful. She is never useless. Always something extraordinarily good happens to her. Ona's husband consults her before he does anything, so I hear."

"And you think that it is natural?" asked Ekecha.

Silence.

"Natural?" repeated Mgbeke.

"You mean that they have given Mr. Sylvester something to eat?"

"Ona's grandfather was a *dibia*, Mgbada is a *dibia*. They know how to do these things."

"I won't argue with you. But you know me, I don't go to church, but I don't trust these *dibias* either."

"There is something in what you have just said. I don't trust them either. But look at the circumstances. Ona is a great embarrassment to her parents and her two grandmothers. No young man from this town would have married her. This man came from nowhere and married her. They now have three children. Contrary to the expectations of everyone, the man is a good husband. So, Ona's parents would do everything to see that she stays in her marriage."

"I don't doubt what you say. Why don't we see such *dibias* as helping us get husbands for our daughters?"

Ekecha laughed with sadness and then said, "I have washed my daughter with herbs as a *dibia* directed that I should."

"I did, too. I took my daughter to the Lake before cockcrow. I used the herbs prescribed and washed her thoroughly. Then I left the herbs and the sponge used on the *ogwe*, as directed. This is before she went back to the convent."

"Two years ago?"

"Exactly two years ago and nothing has happened."

"Mine was done only last year."

"So, you see what I mean?"

"There are good ones and there are bad ones."

"May the good ones come our way!"

"*Ise*."

The women laughed good-humoredly and prepared to go back home. It was not a good day. Suddenly, it threatened to rain. There was lightning. It cut the air so sharply that the women covered their ears with their hands as they expected the accompanying thunder which came in such fury that Mgbeke's heart began to beat very fast.

"Our Mother protect us! Ogbuide we are in your hands. We are only poor fish-sellers. We have not wronged anyone. Please take us home in peace. Take us home safely."

It was better for the women to remain where they were because it was dangerous to venture out into the deep. Their canoe was small, so anything could happen. So, they dragged it onto the shore and sat under the big tree. Mgbeke thought that she should see Mgbada about her daughter. It embarrassed her to no end that she was still unmarried. She wondered why she had not thought of this before now. True, she was skeptical about *dibias*, but from what had been happening in the town, there were good ones like Mgbada and others outside the town that could be recommended. It was true that she had a kind of phobia about *dibias*.

When she was a child, her mother told her a story

about a woman who went to the *dibia* asking him to give her a love potion for her husband so that he would love her more than the other co-wives. She was the second of three wives. The *dibia* concocted the love potion and asked her to put it in the soup when it was her turn to cook for her husband. She was sensible. She prepared the soup with the concoction but instead of giving the soup to her husband, she sent the soup and the pounded yam *foo-foo* to the *dibia*. The next day, the woman heard that the *dibia* had died after eating a meal sent to him by one of his clients. The woman was hysterical.

"My husband, my husband, you would have died, do you hear, you would have died."

She knelt before her husband while she narrated what happened. She brought out the concoction and showed it to everybody, crying with joy,

"My husband, you would have died."

And there was yet another story about bad *dibias*.

There were two young wives who were both fond of their young husband. The man went to school and so he had a good job with the John Holts firm. The man took care of his young wives, but he had a weakness for going out every night and returning in the early hours of the morning. The women could not stop him, so they went to a *dibia* who prepared something for them to give to their husband so that he would stay home. It had a disastrous effect on their husband. A week after the man ate the food in which the medicine was put, he stopped going out. The women congratulated themselves. Two weeks later, the man stopped going to work. The wives were alarmed. "Papa *bomboy*, breakfast is ready, have breakfast and go to work."

No way. The man would not venture out. The older of the two wives called in friends to persuade their husband to go to work. The friends were unable to persuade him. He appeared frightened; he would not go out with them.

"What is the matter?" asked his best friend.

"They said I mustn't go out; I mustn't venture out."

"Who said you mustn't go out?" asked his friend.

"So, they said. I mustn't go out," the crazy husband said.

No *dibia* for Mgbeke. She was not going to indulge in it. She had four co-wives, and five children. If the gods and goddesses agree, her first daughter will marry a rich husband. She would help her bring up her other children. She was not going to marry another man, though there were suitors. A man runs after you when you are in your husband's house. You have not told him that you are looking for a husband. He promises you heaven and earth. If you are foolish, you leave your husband and your children, and go with him. He wants only you, not your children. Your children suffer the indignity that is the lot of such a wayward mother. And you—after a few months, the new husband is tired of his new wife. You take your queue, and you are forgotten.

Yet, whatever happened to Ona and her husband must be investigated. She must see Mgbada and find out exactly what he did. He is a *dibia* after all. He is known to cure ailments. He could, Mgbeke thought, use his magical powers to get a husband for her daughter.

So, she turned to her friend, Ekecha, and said, "I think we should see Mgbada about our daughters, you know."

"I have already made up my mind to see him about my daughter. Let's go home, Mgbeke. Our Mother is not happy with us today."

"What have we done wrong?"

"Mgbada should know. We must go to him."

Mgbada was at home when the women visited. Akpe was not in. It was easier to talk to Mgbada when his wife was away. After breaking the kola nut, he told them why they had come.

"You did well to come to me, Mgbeke and Ekecha. If I were a bad *dibia* I would ask you to bring me the heart of *ndanda*, you know *ndanda*, the smallest of all ants."

The women smiled. "Only quacks demand that. Go home and live in peace with your co-wives."

Silence.

"Is that all?" thought the women.

"We have no quarrel with our co-wives," said Mgbeke.

"I did not say that you quarrel with them. I said live in peace with them."

Silence.

"Are they responsible for our daughters not catching husbands?" Mgbeke asked.

"I did not say so."

Silence.

"How do they come in then?"

Silence.

"I say what I am directed to say."

"So, there is nothing you can do?" Ekecha said.

"I have said something to you. Be at peace with your co-wives."

"Ekecha, let's go home," Mgbeke said, getting up.

"Can you accept our kola nuts?"

"You brought kola nuts for me?"

"Yes," said Ekecha.

"Why should I refuse your kola nuts? Thank you for bringing them."

The women left.

"Just tell me how one can be at peace with one's co-wives?" That was Mgbeke speaking as soon as they were out of earshot.

"We asked for it," said Ekecha.

"Isn't it strange that he has only one wife?" said Mgbeke.

"The work of Mama Theresa."

"Don't say that, Ekecha, Mama Theresa is a Christian, a staunch one at that. If Mgbada, or indeed any man, wants to marry another wife, no force on earth would stop him. He has only one wife because he wants to. The day he wants another, he will have her. No *dibia* can stop that."

"I understand. But you forget that Mgbada's mother is equally formidable. You mean she too wants her son to have just Akpe? Since the birth of Ona... how old is Ona?"

"That's exactly what I am saying. How old is Ona? Mgbada does not want another wife," said Mgbeke.

"He is going to have one in old age. You wait and see."

"This advice to be at peace with our co-wives baffles me," continued Mgbeke. "We came for something important and Mgbada trivialized it all. I don't understand."

"I am in speaking terms with mine," said Mgbeke.

"And so, I am. The youngest, whom our husband married three years ago, cooks for him. So, there is nothing really that I can do. She greets me and I greet her. The other two trade in the Great River."

"The days we were competing are over. Those were the days we were foolish."

"We were not foolish. We were merely young and

thought that by competing we were gaining the upper hand in the struggle to be the favorite of our husbands."

"And you continued to be deceived until your dear husband married another woman. Then it dawned on you that you were wasting your time, and that what you needed to do was take care of your children because they, and not your husband, would take care of you in old age."

"You are right, my sister. I praise women who marry two or three times."

"Some marry five times. You know of Nwabata."

"Nwabata is sick."

"She and her *chi* know what she is looking for in husbands. After the fifth one, one would have thought that she would stop. No. She married the sixth, a man barely out of school."

"Well, she wanted to be his mother."

"His mother? Men only want and respect their own mothers, not their mistresses or wives turned mothers. That's the mistake Nwabata makes."

"And she never learns. You say she had married her sixth."

"Yes, and she mothers him. She pets him. She washes his clothes for him. She lets him use all her *georges* and when members of his age-grade dance, she makes herself so conspicuous before these young men who are old enough to be her sons; it is sickening. I give the marriage two years."

"Two years? That's too long. The third one lasted for only eight months."

"Was it only eight months? I thought it lasted for a year and a half."

"No, eight months."

"Why did she leave him?"

"The man was only after her wealth. And you know she is clever. When she realized what the man wanted, she reacted swiftly. She began to remove her property in a systematic and secret way. She continued to cook for him. There was nothing she could do about that because when she became the man's wife, she was the fourth, and in no time, she edged her co-wives out and took over the cooking completely."

"Poor woman, she did not know what she was in for."

"Her co-wives were amused. They let her go on with her folly. They had been foolish before. A favorite wife has a lot of headaches. She has to have the wherewithal to be able to cope."

"You are telling me. Your husband goes out to drink. Because you are the favorite wife, you wait for him to return. If it is late, you go in search of him. If you are lucky, he is merely tipsy and you beg him to come home with you. He may come with you or he may invite his age-grade to his house. You are in for it. You have to use your own resources to find something for his age-grade to eat and drink. If you are unable to provide these, then you are not a good wife. You are not the favorite."

"A woman should just marry once in her lifetime, that's what I think."

"That is, if she finds fulfilment in the marriage. If not, what does she do?"

"I see what you mean. If the first marriage does not give her children, then perhaps the second would."

"That's what I mean. You know of Ojebo?"

"The daughter of Nwanyiuzo?"

"Yes. She was barely sixteen years old when she married that Beach Master in U.A.C. For five years, she had no child. Her mother pressured her to stay because her husband was wealthy. When she could not bear it any longer, she ran away to Ose Akwa. There she met a young shop attendant who married her. Now she has four children. You see what I mean? So, I really don't blame those who marry many times. But Nwabata's case is different. She is in a class by herself."

"I am thinking seriously about what Mgbada told us," said Mgbeke. "Be at peace with your co-wives."

"Yes. Why should he say that to us? We did not ask him to harm them. We wanted to know why our daughters were still single and what he would do for them to have good husbands. Not just husbands, but good ones."

"You think we should go back to him?" added Ekecha.

"When we are at peace with our co-wives, then we can go back to him."

"I didn't know you were at war with yours," said Ekecha.

"Are you at peace with yours?" The women burst into laughter.

"Aren't women really the cause of the disaffection among women?"

"What man would not be flattered if he had three or more wives competing for his attention?"

"We deserve what we get," said Mgbeke.

"Yes, but don't blame us too much. It is our custom. Look at us, why don't we leave our daughters alone?"

"No, you don't understand me. As I have said many times, a woman should marry. What else is there for us? But we should not make our husbands little gods. Some of us pamper them too much. They become spoilt children; you see what I mean. And when we are…"

"Ekecha."

"Yes."

"I am listening to you. What is it?"

"We must see Ona. We must see Ona, we…"

"We must see Ona? What for?"

"She will 'see' for us. Why haven't I thought of her before? She has extraordinary powers."

"She is a mad woman."

"That's what you think. I am going to see her tomorrow. You remember she and my daughter attended school together. My daughter was one of her bridesmaids. She will tell me one or two things that will help."

"If you think so, we shall see her tomorrow."

Chapter 15

Mr. Sylvester travelled home to see his kith and kin; his parents died when he was a child. He told them that he was about to lose his wife to a Water Goddess. His people were horrified.

"And what are you doing about it?" They asked him.

"I have come to you for advice."

"You want our advice?"

"Yes."

"Here's our advice. Run for your dear life. That is our advice."

"Are you joking?"

"How can you joke with the Goddess of the Water? How can you joke with the Lake People? Didn't we advise you to not marry from among the Lake People?"

"What about my children?"

"Leave your children with them."

"Mm?"

"We say: Leave your wife and children in that place and return home where you belong. We shall find another wife for you. In a matter of five years, you will have five children. Please don't joke with your life. You have only one life. We know that those people have bewitched you. We know that they have given you some love potions to drink. We say: Abandon your wife and children. Your wife is only a wife; she is not your sister. She is not a blood relation. Their ways are not our ways. You must sever all connections. Come home before the water spirit takes you too."

Mr. Sylvester fell silent. Then he said, "There is nothing you can do for us? I am a Christian, you know."

"We are all Christians. But Christianity has nothing to do with this. There is indeed a water goddess. If your wife has something to do with her, that's too bad. All we are saying is this: return to us."

"We were married in church."

"Our son is getting mad," they said. "Those strange people have indeed bewitched you. We have to consult our medicine men."

"Good. Consult them. That's what I want to hear. Consult them."

The people consulted their own medicine men, and the story was the same: "Run for your life."

Another medicine man who was consulted on Mr. Sylvester's insistence said, "By the time you reach home, your wife will be gone."

"Gone where?"

"Wherever the spirit of the Water Goddess took her. My child, there is nothing you can do. You cannot get your wife back. She is not your wife, has never been your wife. It is surprising to me that you are still alive and well and that your business is thriving. Nevertheless, you must abandon your wife. Don't blame her. It is not her fault. She must answer the call. Go back, say goodbye to your in-laws and run. Leave your children with them until they are older. Your in-laws are good people. They will take care of your children. It is not true that your in-laws have bewitched you. Take my advice, my child, and may our ancestors protect you."

"Nothing can be done?"

"Nothing, my child. You are a good man and that's why you are alive to ask these questions. Your hands are clean. Do as I have advised you."

Mr. Sylvester returned to Ugwuta and went to see Mgbada. When he finished talking to him, he cleared his throat. Then he said, "I have heard you. Now listen to me. We are the Lake People."

"The Lake People?"

"Yes, the Lake People. We live on the Lake. We call the Lake Goddess Uhamiri or Ogbuide. We sometimes call her Mother. She is the Mother of all of us. Our forefathers discovered her while they were fishing many years ago. They were fascinated by the Lake's blue waters, fishes, depth and volume of water. They had not seen anything quite like that before. So, they worshipped her for she was a great Goddess. The blue waters of the Lake were awesome and a source of wealth for our forefathers. We believe that the Goddess protects us and inspires us to great heights. We believe that no invader from any part of the world can destroy us. We believe that the deity is a beautiful and ageless woman who is partial to women. We believe that she intervenes in the lives of the people, both men and women, but more especially women. And that's where my daughter, Ona, comes in. But let me tell you more about Ogbuide before I come to my daughter.

"Ogbuide is worshipped like a goddess by her priestesses. As the Christians have Sundays, so does Ogbuide have Orie. Her priestesses are called by her. It is a divine call, and it is for life, and when one is called, one must obey. Failure to obey means disability or even death. The priestess hood does not pass from mother to daughter. So, it is not hereditary, you see."

He paused. He reached for the palm wine in the gourd and poured himself a generous amount in the horn and drank it in one gulp.

"My son-in-law, drink; I say drink. Don't let me drink alone. There is no problem that cannot be solved one way or the other. I have been meaning to say this to you for a long time, but have failed. Not because I did not have the courage, but I had thought that Ona would be rejected by Ogbuide when she married you and had those children. Why, well, let me continue. I regret my presumptuousness; my audacity in believing that Ona could be rejected by the great Woman of the Lake. I ought to have known better, being my father's son, a *dibia* and a diviner of repute. But are we not often partial when we have to deal with problems affecting our blood relations? Perhaps it was my wife and this new religion."

He stopped talking, drank more palm wine and went on. "But why should I blame my wife? Blaming Akpe means that I am weak. I must not blame her. I was wrong in thinking that once Ona married and had children, she would be rejected by our great Mother. I was wrong, painfully wrong. I suspected long ago, in fact as soon as Ona was born, that there was something peculiar about her, something mysterious, unnatural even. It was not revealed to me then that she was not my daughter but the priestess of Ogbuide. That was why I named her Ona, my precious jewel. I loved her right from the time she was inside her mother's womb. Ona was overdue. For twelve months she was in her mother's womb. The mission doctor had wanted to induce labor, but I would hear none of it. My child would be born normally like any other child. So, I took charge of my wife. I refused to listen to my mother. Then the child was born. Akpe had a normal delivery. I rejoiced; I sacrificed to my ancestors and the gods and goddesses. I think that it was partly because of her that I resigned from teaching and faced my profession which is traditional medicine.

"Ona did strange things, disappearing at will and all that. She loved water; she swam in the Lake. She loved to fish. She hated school and was not interested in the Christian religion. We sent her to Father Millet but she returned without being cured. Then you came along and married her. We believed that once she was married, the spirit of Ogbuide would leave her. For a while we were proved right. She was normal again. She became a mother of three children. You came to me when she began to talk to herself. When that happened, I prayed to God and our ancestors; I sacrificed to the gods and the goddesses imploring them to protect my daughter. But I was merely annoying the Spirit of the Lake. She had chosen her among all others, she had been called and there was nothing any human being could do. I should have known better. But maybe my education and Christianity blurred my vision. My wife and her mother must have contributed to my foolishness to think that Ona could escape the call of the great Woman of the Lake. My son-in-law, I must stop. I am repeating myself. This is my daughter's story. She is not mad. She is possessed by the Spirit of the Lake. It is not her fault that she is thus possessed. It is not the fault of her parents either.

Our Mother chose her, called her to do a service for her. Why she was called, I as a medicine man, I as a diviner, cannot tell you. This is the story of my daughter."

"From what you have told me, there is nothing I can do for my wife?" asked the sad Mr. Sylvester.

"I am afraid there is nothing you can do. If there was anything anyone could do, I would have done it long before you married her. You see, our Mother is a jealous deity. She is very demanding. But for me, but for the sacrifices I had performed, the story would have been different."

"So, we can no longer be husband and wife?"

"I am afraid so."

"But we married in the church. The Fathers married us. Surely, they can do something. I want my wife. Ona is my wife. I don't know any spirit called Ogbuide."

"So, you will say, my son."

"And I am right."

"You are right in your own context, my son. There are mysteries upon mysteries in this world."

"What do you advise we do?"

"You and Ona?"

"Yes, my wife and I."

"You cannot run away from the wishes of the Goddess."

"You read my mind."

"I did. You want to leave Ugwuta? Where will you

take Ona to? You must take her where there is water, where when she opens her eyes in the mornings, she would see water."

"I am thinking of Onicha."

"But the Great River is there. There will be no place for Ona and you."

"My God."

They fell silent. Mgbada poured himself another horn of palm wine and drank all of it in one gulp. "Wine has a dual purpose; you drink it when you are happy and when you are sad. Drink, my son-in-law."

He poured a hornful and gave it to Mr. Sylvester. He took it from him, placed it on his lips and drained it. "That's better. That's why we are men. We can drink to drown our sorrows. Another?"

"Yes," replied Mr. Sylvester. But this time he sipped it. Usually, he did not drink much.

"My children," thought Ona's husband. "Who will take care of the children? Tell me, my father, how did you know this? Why are you so sure?"

"My son, but you came to me. You narrated to me the behavior of my daughter. You told me about the unkind words that your neighbors said to you. You told me there were some women who offered their daughters to you in marriage because, as they said, my daughter was a sick woman, a mad woman who should not be allowed to live among normal human beings. You told me about the seizures which were becoming rather frequent, the tendency to cry and shout and behave in an abnormal manner. These are all signs of the call."

"And Ona cannot refuse?"

"I have told you; refusal means disability or death."

"Acceptance?"

"Means security, power and peace."

"Say them again."

Mgbada repeated what he said, "Security… Power… Peace."

Mr. Sylvester said slowly, "Security." Pause. "Power." Pause. "Peace." Ona deserves all three. And how about me, her husband, what will happen to me? Doesn't the deity care about me?"

Silence.

"Doesn't she?"

"This is a difficult question. I have to give it serious thought."

"She should understand."

"Understand?"

"Yes."

"God's ways are not our ways. Ogbuide's ways are not our ways. She calls whomsoever she pleases."

"She does not call husband and wife?"

"How is that possible, my son?"

"Why should she call someone's wife?"

Silence.

"Why?"

Silence.

More silence.

"Let us not, in our lack of understanding and ignorance, annoy the deity. Marriage is for mortals like us. In their own realm, gods and goddesses do not recognize marriage."

"My Ona," Mr. Sylvester said in anguish. "Who am I to compete with the deity? But there must be something in your tradition that can reverse this call, that can make Ona mine and mine alone."

Mgbada shook his head in disagreement.

"So, Ona will now be 'married' to the deity?"

"I am afraid so, and sever sexual relationship with all men."

"All men?"

"All men. Without exception."

"Like the nuns?"

"How right you are. Like the nuns are 'married' to Christ."

"And you say men cannot be her priests?"

"I did not say so. Men can be her priests if they are called."

"If they are called?"

"I can be called for Ona's sake."

"That would be another kind of call; after you would have divorced Ona. A unique kind of call, I should say."

"A late call perhaps?"

"Yes, many, women are called late in life. How I wish Ona had been called late in life. But no, she was called right from the womb. Our goddess is partial to women. I have said this a dozen times."

"Why is this so?"

"Because women are more reliable, I think. I am not sure. Your question is a difficult one, my son-in-law. But I understand your plight."

"Women, more reliable?"

"You doubt me?"

"Men keep secrets. Women don't." Mgbada smiled.

"That is what we say of women. It is like giving a dog a bad name to hang it. No, my son. Women are better than men in keeping the numerous taboos of our Mother. They are endowed with great patience. And remember, priestesses of Ogbuide must abstain from sexual relationship with men. How many of us men could do this?"

Silence.

"The Spirit has killed me."

"No, she has not. You shall get over it. When the gods give us *craw-craw*, they also give us nails with which to scratch."

Chapter 16

Mgbada assembled his wife, Mama Theresa and Nwafor. He wanted to brief them about the new life that Ona was to lead. He said, "I will first start with Ona's husband. I have told him about Ona's calling. He did not take it well. That is understandable. Fortunately, he has brought over the children, and my wife is taking care of them. He has now moved over to Kalabari Beach. He still sees Ona from time to time. This is rather dangerous. I am confident that as time goes on, he will get over the whole thing."

"I want to say something."

"Go on, my mother."

"We must think of marrying a wife for Ona's husband."

Nobody spoke.

She went on, "I say this with great sense of responsibility. Ona's husband is a stranger in Ugwuta.

He has now moved over to the other side of the Lake, Kalabari Beach. There are many strangers there. They are going to influence him one way or the other as time goes on. We can hold him; we can be close to him if we give him another wife. You see…"

"But they were married in church. The church does not allow this sort of thing."

"My daughter," said Mama Theresa, "we all go to this church. We all must be realistic about this church. We are dealing with an abnormal situation which needs an abnormal solution. I agree with you, my namesake."

Akpe was silent.

"As I was saying, we have to do this. This girl we want to be our son-in-law's new wife may not necessarily be educated or be a Christian."

"No!" shouted Akpe.

"Keep cool, my wife."

"I won't keep cool. You are pagans and non-believers. I don't know what you are doing. You have destroyed my daughter. You are now proceeding to destroy my son-in-law. You have driven him away from this town. Is that not enough for you?"

Nobody spoke for a long time.

"I am going to the mission. I am going to see the priest. I am not going to live with you anymore. I am not your wife anymore."

"Take it easy, my daughter. We are all Christians.

There are traditions; there are cultures. We can blend these traditions and cultures with the Christian culture. Sit down, my daughter, and listen to your husband. Don't behave like Madam Margaret. We all know that she has gone nuts in the name of Christian religion."

Akpe sat down and grumbled, but said nothing.

"As I was saying, we must think of marrying a wife for Ona's husband," Nwafor continued. "I have someone in mind. She is the daughter of my childhood friend. She did not go to school, and that makes it easier. If you agree with me, allow me to go about it the way I think fit."

All fell silent.

Then Mgbada said: "We agree with you, go ahead. Over to our daughter, Ona. I have done everything that was expected of me. Ona has been properly initiated into the priesstesshood of Ogbuide. I have built a hut for her on my own plot of land, not far from us. Her life has changed drastically. We all must accept it and help her to play her role."

"Then of course, we shall take care of her children. She will not have time now to look after them. My mother has arranged for a little girl who will help Akpe take care of Ona's children. Does anyone have anything to say?"

Nobody had anything to say, so they dispersed.

Ona had three huts.

One comprised of a bed and sitting room, and the other a large room where she kept all the paraphernalia of her office. The third one, which was tiny, was used as her kitchen. The huts were built of red mud and thatched roofs—Mgbada made sure that the best materials were used. Ona rubbed the walls with red earth, and the floor with well-ground charcoal. She decorated the walls with plates of different colors and sizes. The kitchen contained just the fireplace and *uko* where she dried her fish, spices, herbs and vegetables. There was a large earthenware pot in the kitchen. Sometimes her children fetched water for her and filled the large pot. She also had two low stools and mortars which she used in pounding yam *foo-foo*. The small one she used for the pepper and other spices.

The sitting room was quite large. She had mud benches built on three sides of the walls. Beautiful mats were spread on the mud benches. There were no chairs or stools in the sitting room. The bedroom contained a bamboo bed with a mat spread on it. There was a mud wardrobe on the opposite side of the bed. In the mud wardrobe were kept iron pots, jars of different sizes and boxes containing valuables. On the top of the wardrobe were pots, pans and plates that were not used frequently. At one end of the bedroom was an earthenware pot filled with the lake water. Ona had used white clay to rub on the earthenware pot, so that it was all white. Pieces of red and white cloths were tied round the pot. Next to the pot was a kola nut dish which contained two kola nuts, a piece of white clay, a feather of a parrot and *edo*. This part of the room was her shrine. When she woke up each morning, she knelt down before the shrine and worshipped the Goddess. She broke a kola nut, gave to the Goddess and bit off a little piece. Then she fetched a bottle of *kai kai*, gave to the spirit, and sipped a little.

It was after this ritual that she came out to be seen. Ona lived alone in her huts. Her children fetched her water and firewood when they were able. She cooked her food herself. She did not eat food that was cooked by someone else. When her children visited her, she played with them, gave them baths when needed, fed them and gave them snacks, such as groundnuts and fruits in season. She went to the market on Nkwo and bought and sold.

On ordinary days she attended to her numerous clients. She did some gardening around the house. On Eke nights she was possessed by the Spirit of the Water. She danced to the music only she alone heard. She was sometimes in a trance and made predictions or gave messages from the spirit world to people. She sometimes fasted when she was ordered to do so. She sometimes knocked her head on the wall or on the ground, rolling over and over. No one interfered, for she was doing what the Goddess had commanded her to do.

On Orie, she devoted the entire day to the worship

of Ogbuide. She killed a white hen or cock, sacrificed parts of it to the Goddess and prepared the rest for the children or whoever was around at the time. Orie was a work-free day. She communicated with the spirits and the Goddess on this day. She ate only unripe plantains on this day. She invoked the Goddess and prayed for peace.

On Afor, Ona received clients from different walks of life. They consulted her on a number of issues—good health, childlessness, riches and long life. She had more female than male clients. They sought her advice on a number of issues, such as ways to deal with their husbands and co-wives. Ona's clients, in return for these services, presented her with gifts according to their abilities. Some brought her kola nuts, alligator pepper, and different kinds of fruits. Others gave her goats, sheep, cocks and yams; never cocoyam or cassava. She shared these gifts with her family. She kept the goats and the sheep and this was how she got to have many sheep and goats, which she sold to keep body and soul together; for she was not allowed to charge fees for consultation.

Ona, even in this position, went to mass, but she did not receive Holy Communion. Her mother was so upset about her calling that she blamed everybody for Ona's fate. Try as she could, Ona could not convince her that no one but the Spirit of the Lake was to blame. Akpe, on her own part, was unable to accept her daughter's call. She prayed. She fasted. She virtually lived in the mission, praying and ministering to God and the Fathers, hoping that God would reverse the fate of her daughter. Akpe so carried on that the people feared that her behavior could lead to insanity. She muttered to herself while going to the mission with a chaplet in hand. Her mother tried to help, but failed, for Akpe refused all help. At this time, she had stopped cooking for her husband and her mother could not get her to rescind her decision. Mgbada was tolerant to a fault. He pleaded but to no avail.

"You are weak," his mother admonished.

"I know what I am doing, mother."

"You do not know. Marry another woman now and you will see the difference."

"It will not solve my problem."

"What is your problem?" asked Mgbada's mother.

"I don't want any distractions. I want to see my daughter through."

"See your daughter through? I don't understand you."

"She needs my help."

"I can understand that. And then?"

Silence.

"Marry another wife and end this bluff. Why won't Akpe cook for you? Why?"

Silence.

"It wasn't you that called Ona to the priestesshood. Why should she take it out on you?"

"I know what I am doing, mother."

"I say you don't. All right, tell me what you mean by distractions."

Silence.

"Mgbada, you have only two sons."

"There are many who don't have any."

"So, you won't marry another wife."

"I have not said so."

"Well then?"

"It is not my priority."

"What is your priority?"

"My daughter, Ona, the priestess of Ogbuide. I must see her through."

"But that's what you are doing."

"I know. She needs my support. Her children need my support. A wife now would bring distraction."

Chapter 17

It was Eke. Ezemiri, Queen of Water—as Ona was now called—woke up as usual at the first cock crow. She lifted her earthenware pot effortlessly onto her head, for she was of average height, and went down to the Lake. There was no one at the Lakefront. So, she undressed and waded into the water. She immersed herself in the water. It was fresh and cool. Then she went to the *ogwe*, where she scrubbed herself with a sponge and black soap. She rinsed her body and dived into the water. She reappeared with a fistful of the sand of the Lake: "As I bathe in your water, I also take your sand, Ogbuide, the kind Spirit. I greet you this Eke morning. May the day bring us nothing but good fortune!"

She dried herself, put on her clothes, balanced the earthenware pot on her head and went home. Since Ona became the priestess of Ogbuide, she wore only white and red clothes, and covered her hair with either blue or red head-tie. On this Eke morning, she took care of her makeup. She rubbed coconut oil all over her body. Then she rubbed a mixture of the coconut oil and camwood. She combed her long hair and braided it instead of plaiting it with black thread. For effect, she rubbed clay on her feet, on her forehead and on the back of her hands. When she finished, she came out and sat in her sitting room, as if she was expecting some visitors. Ona's three pregnancies and three children did not leave any mark on her. She was thin and agile and still retained her fair complexion. She was precise and fast. But when she talked, she took her time. She spoke slowly and weighed her words, pausing for a considerable length of time for good effect.

She stood up from her chair and looked around. Her rooms had been swept, the kitchen and the compound, too. She was going to have her first meal at noon. Her eyelids twitched.

"Visitors," she said. "I am going to have visitors today. Ogbuide be praised. May my visitors come in peace! May I be in a position to take care of their needs!"

Ezemiri then busied herself putting things in order. She went into the room, brought out a lobe of kola nut and threw it on the ground. She went back, fetched the bottle of *kai kai*, poured a generous amount into a glass, and poured it on ground for the ancestors to drink.

"Are they coming from afar?" she asked. "Oh, good,

from Ugwuta? Ogbuide be praised. I am waiting for them," she said.

Ezemiri went back to her sitting room. She sat down, took a piece of white clay, *edo* and a feather. First, she called on the Supreme God thus:

> *Supreme God*
> *The creator of all things*
> *The creator of*
> *The Lake Goddess*
> *Whom I serve*
>
> *Supreme God*
> *The creator of Water*
> *Land*
> *Air*
> *The Lake Goddess*
>
> *Lake Goddess*
> *Who lives underneath*
> *The blue Lake*
> *You who mingle in water*
>
> *You who are one*
> *With water*
> *You whom I serve*

The Water Goddess
You are water
Without water
We die
Without water
We are nothing

Ogbuide,
You taught me
From my mother's womb
To worship you

To use your water
To cure
All diseases
Because water is life
Without water
The fishes of the Lake
Would die
Without water
The plants in the forest
Would die
Without water
We humans
Would die

Great Goddess
The Supreme God
Made you great
By making you
The Water Goddess

Ogbuide, the Lake Goddess
You chose me
From my mother's womb
To serve you and
To be your priestess
Therefore Ogbuide
I must be your priestess
Until I die.

Ogbuide, the Lake Goddess
You gave me power
Before I was born
To do your will
Therefore, I must do your will

Ogbuide, the Lake Goddess
The beautiful woman
Ogbuide
The hairy woman
Ogbuide
The owner of water

Ogbuide
The kind spirit
How can I reject you?
Can anyone reject
Water
And live?
Can anyone reject
Air
And live?
Can anyone reject
Land
And live?
Ogbuide
You are all three.

Ogbuide
Therefore
I will continue
To serve you
Using this white clay
Using this edo
Using this feather

You have given me the power
You have revealed to me
The leaves
The roots

The herbs
To cure the sick
I will continue
To use them
To the glory of
Your name

Ogbuide, the Lake Goddess
You have not
Given me power
To harm anyone
Therefore, I will never
Harm anyone.
Strike me dead
With your huge fan
Strike me dead
By lightning
By thunder
If I should harm anyone

Ogbuide, the Lake Goddess
I said to my mother:
Mother
Accept me as
I am
Ogbuide has chosen me
I said to my mother:

Beat me
Kick me
Starve me
Put me in jail
I only know one deity
That deity Is Ogbuide

I must continue
To worship you
To sacrifice to you
To keep holy your day

I must continue
To be upright
In my thoughts
And in my deeds
I must do
What you command
Me
To do

You charge me
To help everyone
Who comes to me
For help I promise
I shall help all of them
The sick

The afflicted
The hopeless
The women
Yes, your fellow women

They have a special Place
In your abode
Underneath the Lake

Ogbuide, the Lake Goddess
You have chosen me
Who am I?
That you should
Choose me?

Good woman
I leave all in
Your hands
I wait for
Your command
Ogbuide,
Our Mother.

When Ona finished, she took a kola nut from the dish and broke it. There were three lobes. She nodded. She threw one lobe outside for the ancestors. Then she gave one to Ogbuide. She took one herself and bit off a little piece. She cleared her throat noisily. She went inside her room and came out again. Then she heard her father's voice from afar.

"He must have gone out early;" she thought.

"*Mazi*," she greeted him as he came near.

"*Ada bu ada, ezi ada*, Ezemiri. You look so gorgeous this morning."

"Father, welcome, sit down and eat kola and drink some *kai kai*."

"You say so?"

"I say so."

Father and daughter laughed. Ona brought another kola nut in a dish with some dried fish and one penny and placed it in front of her father.

"My daughter, all this for me?"

"All for you, my father. You deserve much more than this. I have not cooked."

Mgbada took the kola nut, evoked the spirits of the ancestors and Ogbuide, broke it and took a lobe.

"The money is for breaking the kola," Mgbada said as he took the one penny and put in his pocket.

They talked about a variety of subjects. Mgbada was doing well in his job as a diviner and a medicine man. He farmed and fished. He was contented.

"I want to tell you something." He paused.

"Go ahead, father, I am all ears."

"Be kind to your husband."

"I am kind to him."

"I know you are."

They fell silent.

"Wasn't he here the other day?"

"Yes, he was here."

"And what happened?"

She said nothing.

Mgbada sipped the *kai kai*. "Tell me what happened."

"He still does not understand."

"Tell me what happened?" Mgbada repeated.

Ona told her father, and when she finished, he remained silent for a long time.

"I have told him to leave."

"You have?"

"I had to, father. I don't want Ogbuide to be angry with him."

"He is a good man."

"I know, father."

"He is taking it badly."

Long silence.

"And his children are good children. Akpe is taking good care of them. She makes sure they go to school and catechism."

"Catechism? Of course."

"I want us to do something," began Mgbada.

"I am listening, father."

"We want to get a wife for your husband."

"Father," Ona exclaimed, "I thought of it last night."

"You did?"

"Yes, my father."

"You are a good daughter. Why do I have to share you with the Water Goddess?"

Ona frowned.

"Don't mind me. We have given a thought to a wife for your husband. And we have in mind the daughter of Onyenye."

"Onyenye? I don't know her."

"Onyenye is your mother's friend and a not-too-distant relation."

"I am listening."

"We must not allow your husband to leave us, because of your children. Your children are staying with us now, but I know that sooner than later, he would get over his problem and leave us, taking the children with him, whereas if we get a wife for him, he and the children will remain with us."

"I agree, father. I leave you to make inquiries and also convince my husband. What about mother, have you talked to her?"

"She does not approve. She is too involved in the mission. I fear for her."

They fell silent.

"The Catholic church will not approve. God joined you and your husband together for better or for worse. The Goddess of the Lake has put you asunder. You know your mother. I must go home. Your husband must have a wife. My mother is seeing to it."

"I agree with you, father."

"I must go now. The day is far spent." Mgbada got up. "It seems as if you are going to have visitors," he said, taking one step.

"You feel it, or the visitors are in sight?" Ona said, also standing up.

"They are in sight. I must go now."

Chapter 18

"Mgbeke and Ekecha, welcome. Two friends, you are like sisters. Welcome. Come over here and sit down," Ona said, ushering in the two women.

"Our Ona, thank you," Ekecha said, sitting down. She continued, "My friend and I thought it wise to see you today. Did you receive our message?"

"Your message? You sent me a message to tell me you would come today?"

The two women nodded in agreement.

Ona laughed. "That's too formal, my sisters, too formal. You gave the message to my mother, I presume?"

"Yes." the two women answered.

"Akpe, my mother. She did not deliver the message. You know her; she belongs to the God of the Christians. I belong to the Goddess of the Lake. She is not happy that I did not go to school and that I am now a priestess. My poor mother! I have tried my best to make her understand. But my calling is too much for her. I don't blame her. Sometimes I ask myself, why me? Welcome."

"So, Ona, you no longer go to church?" asked Mgbeke.

"No, I don't go any more. I used to go, but I discovered that my mind was not in it. I was called to greater things. Rather than go for mass every Sunday and listen to rubbish and see people who have no business whatsoever being in the church, because of their bad ways, kneel down in front of the altar and receive the Holy Communion, I stay home. I call on our ancestors; I go to the waterfront and call on the great Spirit of the Lake. I entreat them to help me solve my problems and the problems of those who come to me. I am confident that the ancestors and the Goddess of the Water will answer my prayers."

"So, you have fallen by the wayside?" Mgbeke said smiling; she has a good sense of humor.

"Yes, I have given my chaplet to Akpe."

"You have?" continued Mgbeke.

"Yes, so she can pray for the two of us, while I devote my time to the worship of Ogbuide. Look at me talking. I have not offered you kola nuts."

"Don't worry, our Ona."

"Meaning what? I have kola nut," she said and went into the bedroom to fetch it. They ate kola nut and talked about a variety of things. Ona offered them *kai kai*, they refused, but she persuaded them to drink palm wine instead.

"I heard that Onyemuru had left her husband and married another man," said Ona.

The two women laughed.

"Isn't it true?"

"It is true."

"Why do you laugh then?"

"Because it will not last."

"She is looking for a male child."

"And she thinks that she will have a male child by marrying another man."

"She is right."

"Right?"

"She can be lucky with the new husband. You cannot rule that out."

"You are right, Ona," said Mgbeke.

Turning to her friend, she said, "We are forgetting Ojiuzo."

"Of course, Ojiuzo who had four girls in a row. Her mother-in-law nearly killed her. So, she left her husband and married Chukwudifu. Her first child with Chukwudifu was a boy, second and third were also boys."

"Really?" Ona said.

"It happened in this town," said Ekecha. "The only difference between Onyemuru and Ojiuzo is that the former had had three previous marriages…"

The women laughed. Mgbeke cleared her throat. It was time to say why they were visiting Ona. "We have come to you."

"Welcome."

"It is about our daughters." She paused and continued, choosing her words. "Our daughters should have been married by now but have not. And we are worried."

Ona nodded.

"We have done everything," added Ekecha.

There was a long silence.

Then Ona asked, "What and what have you done?"

The women kept silent.

"Tell me what you have done, perhaps it will help me."

The women did not want to say what they had done. So, they remained silent.

"Give me a moment," Ona said.

She left the women in the sitting room and went to the back of the house.

"We mustn't tell her," whispered Mgbeke to Ekecha.

"Of course not," replied Ekecha.

"Perhaps she has gone for consultations," said Mgbeke.

"With these priestesses, one never knows. We have come. We have to see it through."

"Don't mention her father," warned Mgbeke.

"Am I a fool? Don't I have common sense?"

Ona returned to the sitting room. She said, "Welcome, my fellow women; welcome. I have heard you. How old are your daughters?"

"My daughter was born the year Okwuonye died and my friend's daughter, a month after Okwuonye's death."

"Okwuonye Maduka."

"The same one," said Mgbeke.

"My grandmother told me about her. She was a woman of rare gifts."

"That's Okwuonye, a woman of rare gifts."

"Her death shook Ugwuta and environs."

"So, it did."

"I was told that she was a very wealthy woman."

"She was wealthy. Her great grandfathers and grandmothers traded with the white people when they first came. When I say white people, they were not those who built their trading posts at the 'company'—I mean those who came in ships from across the Great River."

"The Potokiri?"

"Yes, the Potokiri."

"She made a lot of money but did not want to get married. Her mother was a strong woman, too, so she compelled her to marry. She married and had a daughter."

"They said she had no child," said Ekecha.

"That is not true. She had a daughter. The problem was that she just could not be a wife to the man who was her husband. She was too strong, too intelligent for her husband. Do you know that she bought things in multiples of two hundred? When she bought canoes, she bought two hundred at a time. When she bought slaves, she bought two hundred at a time. How could she live with a husband who seemed to have nothing?"

"What happened to her wealth when she died?"

"Her daughter and the slaves inherited her wealth."

"The slaves?"

"Yes, the slaves. There were two of them who were loyal to her until her death. So, they benefited from her wealth."

"Slaves don't inherit," said Ona.

"Yes, but when you have loyal ones, you bequeath them something."

"Didn't her husband inherit her property?"

"No, her husband died before her."

"Then the husband's first son should have inherited her property and not her daughter. That is the custom of our people."

"You are right, but as I told you, she was clever. She divorced her husband before he died and went back to her father's house," said Mgbeke.

"Very clever," said Ona.

"She saw how her husband's children were behaving. So, she took the step in order that her own daughter would inherit all her wealth."

"So, if you divorce your husband before he dies or before you die, he has no claim to your property?" asked Ekecha.

"Exactly. You have severed the relationship; you are no longer married to him. So, your property is no longer his or his children's."

"This is a good custom," said Ekecha.

"For you who are still married," said Ona.

"You are no longer married?"

"No, I am now married to the Goddess. Everything I own now belongs to the Goddess."

"So Okwuonye divorced her husband for that purpose?" asked Ekecha.

"Maybe for other reasons as well; who knows? It is a long time. It was said at the time that she hated to wear black, so remaining as a wife meant that she would wear black when her husband died. She did not want to do that."

"She had a voice," said Ona.

"Only a woman who had a voice could do what she did," said Ekecha.

"Ogbuide wants every woman to have a voice. Women should not be voiceless. Ogbuide hates voiceless women," said Ona. She went on:

"This is why the Goddess whom I serve calls certain women to be her priestesses—she, the Goddess, communicates with her fellow women. That is why, Mgbeke and Ekecha, I am happy that you have come to me today. Your daughters are not that old, though. Of course, I understand your anxiety. I am the same age as your daughters and I have married and have three children. And you must realize that education could keep women from marrying early. But I must tell you that I am all for this education. Though I also believe that a woman should have a husband in order to have children. If she does not marry, how can she have children?"

"You say the truth, marriage is important. But our daughters don't have to marry anybody for the sake of marriage."

"We say the same thing, my fellow women. Education is good for our daughters and my own daughter must be educated, though I am not educated myself."

"You are lucky, you married a good man," said one of the women.

"Yes, he is the best husband any woman can have," Ona agreed.

"Your calling must have given him a great blow."

"Yes, he finds it hard to accept my calling."

"Any husband would, but you must do something to soften the blow."

"Like what?"

"Like marrying another wife for him."

"My friend is right," added Mgbeke.

"Get a girl close to you for your husband."

"He will be happy. Ogbuide will also be happy," said Ekecha.

"I have heard you. I shall think about it. I want to go back to this education. I want you to realize that education is very important. Look around and you will see those prominent men who sent their sons and daughters to school. Their daughters have married men who work with the white people. So, I don't have anything against education for our daughters."

"Neither do I. It is just that they spend too much valuable time in school. They should spend less time."

"I see your point, but education is good, the time spent notwithstanding, I regret not going to school."

"You should have gone, Ona. What happened?" asked Mgbeke.

"You know what happened; so don't ask me," Ona said laughing. "And besides," she continued, "I hated school."

"I hated school too, especially the teacher's whip," said Ekecha.

"Me too. I was afraid of the teacher's whips. But what really made me decide to not continue schooling were my brothers and sister. They made fun of me singing: Ona, *onye ujo akwukwo*, Ona, *onye ujo akwuko*. Perhaps if they did not laugh at me, I would have at least known how to read and write. So don't regret sending your daughters to school."

"Ona, you see, we are worried about our daughters because we spend so much money on them."

"You pay the school fees for your daughters' education?"

"We pay for our daughters and sons."

"Your husbands don't pay?"

"At first my husband was responsible for the school fees only. I was responsible for the other expenses like books, uniforms and levies. But when he married another wife, he told me that he was no longer going to pay the fees. So, I paid all the fees. I had no choice. My sons are young. I know I am making a good investment. If my daughter marries well, then she can help me with the others."

"Our husbands are foolish. Why don't they see that the world is changing? Why don't they see the children of Chief Onumonu Uzoaru and learn from him? He married many wives but he sent all his children, both male and female, to school."

"Yes, he did. But you must remember that when he died, those of his wives who could afford it continued to send their sons and daughters to school outside our town. So, our husbands, because the wives of Chief Uzoaru took up this responsibility, thought that other wives who did not have the means must do the same even when their husbands were alive and well."

"And they wonder why mothers are more attached to their sons and daughters."

"*Bia zuru ni azu ego nioo.*"

"Those children have come again," said Mgbeke.

"No, Mgbeke, it is early. This one is genuine."

"*Bia zuru ni azu ego nioo.*"

"Come, my child, bring the fish. I want to buy."

The child brought a basin full of prawns and placed it in front of the women.

"She supplies prawns to me," said Ona.

"I thought she was the child that 'sold' mumps to my son."

Mgbeke proceeded to tell the story to the great amusement of Ona.

"Price the prawns for me, Mgbeke and Ekecha, you go to the market every day."

The women made a good bargain and Ona paid less than what she would have paid if the fish-sellers had not been around.

"What are you going to do with the prawns?"

"I shall dry some and eat some raw. It is my favorite fish since I was a child."

"Do you eat it because you are a priestess or are you merely fond of it?"

"I am fond of it and it agrees with me."

"Tell us about your call. What is it like to be a priestess of Ogbuide?"

"It is hard work." There was no hesitation at all in her reply.

"Hard work?"

"Hard work. Our Mother is very demanding. There are so many things you mustn't do. There are so many taboos, which if you inadvertently break, you pay dearly. So, when I displease her, I make sacrifices. When I sin against her, I atone for my sins. I fast, I pray, I beg her to forgive me."

"There are advantages of course?"

"There are. You have come to me. I am duty-bound to help you solve your problem. So, I have that power which you don't have; and which is why you came to consult me. I have heard you. She will reveal to me now, or some other time, how I can help you."

"It is a good job."

Ona said nothing.

"Would you rather not be her priestess?"

"I have no choice in the matter. If she says I should not be from today, she has said it and I must obey her. I am entirely in her hands."

"I know women who are her friends," said Ekecha.

"There are women who want to be close to her. They consult a diviner or a medicine man and they are told what to do. But whether you are called, or are a friend, the most important thing you will do to be close to her is to keep her days holy; to eat certain foods on her holy day and praise her name. She is a great spirit."

Ona got up as if she heard someone calling her name. She listened, smiled, and waited expectantly.

The women were surprised.

Then she said, "I hear you. I am all ears, go on and give me your command."

She changed her position. Her countenance assumed a pensive look. Then she closed her eyes. She took a step and stopped. Then she took another step. She waited expectantly again. Then she said:

"Yes, I am sitting down. You asked me to sit down. I hear you. If you want me to stand up, just say so. All right. I should sit down. I am all ears. I hear you. Yes, they are here. You have a message for them? Give me the message."

She turned to Ekecha and Mgbeke and said:

"The beautiful one is happy with you. She greets you."

The fish-sellers nodded. "I sing your praises every day."

> *Beautiful woman*
> *Hairy woman*
> *Ageless woman*
> *Mother of all mothers*
> *Owner of the Lake*
> *Owner of the fishes*
> *Owner of the People*
> *Of the Lake*
> *Protector of the*
> *Lake People*
>
> *Ogbuide*
> *Uhamiri*
> *Ezemiri*
> *Queen Mother*
> *Goddess of the Water*
> *Goddess of the fishes*
>
> *The Goddess of thunder*
> *The Goddess of lightning*
> *The protector of women*
> *The Lake Goddess*

Your priestess
Salutes you
Your fellow women
Salute you
They are here before you
Imploring you
To come to their help
I beseech you
Good Mother
Give them
Your abundant
Blessings
Show them the light
Through me
Your priestess

I did not choose myself
You chose me
Give me power
To help these women
My fellow women
They are ordinary women
Only fish-sellers
Be gracious to them
Through me

You gave me power
You revealed to me

The herbs
The plants
The roots
For effective cure

The greatest
Of what you gave me
Is water
Water cures all ills
Water is powerful
And you are water
Water is life
Life is water.

I hear you, I answer
Give me the message.

Silence. The fish-sellers were silent. They heard nothing. But they were aware of Ogbuide's presence. They felt it in their bones.

Their hearts were beating irregularly. Mgbeke's heart missed a beat, Ekecha's beat faster and faster. Should they run? Run to where? Then Ezemiri began:

"Mgbeke and Ekecha, hear Ogbuide's voice. Hear Ogbuide's message. The great one said I should tell you that you have not given her a drink. She is thirsty. Give her a drink so she can quench her thirst."

She paused. She was now standing erect. Her eyes

were closed. She did not look human. She was no longer the woman who was talking with the fish-sellers so familiarly a while ago.

"Ogbuide said, you have not given her a drink," Ezemiri bellowed. "Give her a drink, I say…"

It was Mgbeke who recovered first. She said:

> *Ogbuide, the thunder*
> *Ogbuide, the lightning*
> *The destroyer of our enemies*
> *We salute you*
> *Please forgive us*
> *We are only fish-sellers*
> *We do not know much*
> *We are only children*
> *In your presence*
>
> *Hear us*
> *We brought drinks*
> *Kai kai and palm wine*
> *We brought kola nuts*
> *We brought white clay*
> *We brought edo*
> *We brought feathers*
> *Of ugo*
> *Of the eagle*
> *Of the parrot*
> *We brought*
> *Alligator pepper*

We are children
But we are also Adults
So, how can we
Being children and Adults
Venture near your
Presence
Empty-handed

Nobody sees
A child's tooth
Empty-handed
Our ancestors forbid
We know what
Is expected of us
So, please forgive us

But you must know
Why it appeared
That we neglected
Our duty

We were overwhelmed
By our sister's reception
A good and worthy sister
Whom you chose
Above all others
To be your priestess
We were carried away

Our Mother
Carried away by the
Goodness of our sister

So here is your drink:
Kai kai and palm wine.
We brought Schnapps
As well
All the things in this basin
Are for you and the
Creatures of the Blue Lake

Ogbuide
Queen Mother
We are not strangers
To this land
We know the misery
Of you and your people
We know how you
Fought for us
How you vanquished
All our enemies
We know…

"Pour out the drink now, so that Ogbuide may drink," Ezemiri interrupted Mgbeke. Her eyes were still closed. Her face was calm. There was no sign of strain. She still stood erect. For a while nothing happened. Still with her eyes closed, Ezemiri said,

"*Haa*, father, you came just in time."

Her father entered. "Is that so, my daughter? You have visitors. There are so many things here. Am I welcomed by Ogbuide, or is this a women only gathering?"

"Father, pour the drinks so that Ogbuide may drink. She is thirsty. She is with us. Can't you see her?"

"My daughter, our eyes have gone dim, we no longer see what we should see. Ogbuide, you are welcome to my daughter's home. I salute you. You know why you chose my daughter to be your priestess."

Mgbada took the bottle of *kai kai* and was about to open it when Ezemiri protested

"No, open the bottle of Schnapps."

He opened the bottle of Schnapps, and poured libation invoking Ogbuide and the ancestors to drink. He poured a little for himself, drank it in one gulp and then poured for the women and they drank.

"Ahaa, that's the kola nut. I should have broken it first."

"No, father. Ogbuide wanted to drink first."

"As Ogbuide wishes. I was in time to perform this function. I leave you with your fellow women. Mgbeke and Ekecha, I am going."

He was gone. Ezemiri began:

"We have given drinks to our Mother. Now listen to the rest of the message. Ogbuide said to tell you that she has no quarrel with you. She is pleased with you. You are good wives and you are good mothers. She has given you much, and she expects much from you. In order that all will be well for you, you are each to sacrifice to her a white ram and a white hen. Sacrifice these on Orie. You know her path, the way she takes to Nkwo market, just before you take the right turn to the Lakefront—there, sacrifice these to her before the first cockcrow."

"Ogbuide commanded me to tell each of you to give a goat to your ancestors and to make a feast for the *umuada* in your respective villages, so that the *ikenga* you took with you to your husbands' homes would remain with you and not be taken away from you. If you do all these things, said Ogbuide, you will prosper even as fish-sellers, and your co-wives will not see your back."

"I am here. I hear you. I am giving them the message. All right. I understand."

She turned to the women:

"Ogbuide is here, in your midst, over there. I see her clearly; she is smiling at you. She has her staff of office in one hand and a fan in the other hand. She is dry and wet at the same time. One day she will give you another pair of eyes with which to see her."

"Now, about your daughters. Before the next new yam festival, your daughters will be engaged to worthy men; rich and influential. I have seen the two young men. They are from this town but they live far away. They will come home for the New Yam Festival, and they will look around for wives. They will meet your daughters in a dance arena. So, when your daughters return on holiday, ask them to visit me, or bring them to me. I want to know them well in order to advise them on how to behave when they meet their young men."

"My friends, Ogbuide is with you. She wants you to be friends. She wants you to keep holy her days. She wants you…"

"She is gone. Did you hear her go? Didn't you hear the thunder? Didn't you see the lightning? Never mind. When the time comes, your eyes will be washed with the lake water and herbs—then you will see."

"One more message: Ogbuide said that you should live in peace with everyone. Do not curse anyone, especially children. Ogbuide said…"

She trailed off. She began to recite some incantations. At first slowly, then the incantations came in fits and starts, loud, then inaudible. She slowed down. She opened her eyes and staggered to her seat. She sat down again and closed her eyes. She was exhausted. She began to fan herself with one end of her *wrappa*. It was not fanning her effectively. She took a fan and began to fan herself. Then she began to sing slowly:

Ogbuide
Wherever you lead me
I shall follow you
Going and coming
I shall follow you
Up and down
I shall follow you
Right or left
I shall follow

The fish-sellers joined her, and they sang along:

We shall follow water
Water is life
We shall follow water
Water is life
Life is water
Children of water
Let us pray
To the Queen of Water
Our Goddess
Let us follow our Goddess
Queen of Water
Water will lead us
Water will return us safely

Water is the life of fish
Follow water, we must

Those who believe in water
Those who believe in the Goddess
Great reward will be yours

Mother, superior Mother
Good water, peaceful water

We have come
We have trust in you
We have come, good water
Mysterious water, deep water
We have come

Ogbuide, Queen Mother
Our good Mother
Come closer
Queen of the Lake
Come closer
The Great River
Come closer
Our Mother, come closer
Deep water, come closer
Give us our share
Our share is long life
The lives of our children
The lives of our husbands
Our share is wealth

Our share is children
Our share is happiness
Our share is contentment

Ogbuide, we thank you
Queen of Water, we thank you
Great Mother, we thank you
Good and kind Mother
Come closer
Mother and water are the same
Without water
Who can live?
Without Mother
Who can live?
Our beautiful Mother
Come closer.

The End

Glossary

Ofo (A title, a symbol of truthfulness)
Those who embraced the new religion were becoming distinguished. Mgbada's father knew that he was losing his grip on his first son and so before he died, he charged Mgbada (Antelope) thus: "Whatever you do, whatever you become, don't forget the worship of our ancestors. You have the *ofo* of our family. You are the first son. Much is expected of you. You must carry on after me."

"I, too, I am a Christian. I go to church. I receive the Holy Communion. But I still hold the *ofo* of my ancestors. "

Ana eji (you can't compare/mistake), akpu (body growth), naagbayani (compare/mistake), ara (breast). (You can't compare/mistake body growth to/for breast.)
"Isn't she a smashing daughter?" said one of Akpe's (Mgbada's wife) cousins.

"She is, she is, that's why our brother has gone all out for her," said one of Mgbada's cousins.

"I bet you don't have such daughters in your village," Akpe's cousin said.

"We do, my in-law, we do; keep your eyes open and you will see them—look, there's one over there. How does she compare with yours? Mgbada's cousin asked.

"*Chaasa* (neglect). No comparison, *anaejiakpunaagbayaniara*?" said Akpe's cousin.

"Look, man, mind what you say here; or…" That was Mgbada's cousin. "Look at this man from the farm; don't you have a sense of humor?"

Abumi (I am) okeyi (elder) chi (Spirit) (I am an Elder by birth/creation)

"The king's kola is in the king's hand, so break it," said Nwafor (Mgbada's mother). "No, my namesake, break the kola. You are in my house; I give you the power to break it. I know that I am older than you are."

"Well, if it is that, I am not going to break the kola. You are not older than me."

"We are in the same age-grade."

"Yes, of course," agreed Mama Theresa. "But that does not mean that you are older than me"

"When were you born?"

"Let's not go into that again. Our mothers settled it before they died. Mother said that she and your mother were pregnant during the New Yam Festival. Their age-grade teased them and made predictions on who would give birth first. I came first. Your mother and father went to Aguleri (town) to buy seed yams; it was when they returned that you were born. Therefore, *abumiokeyi chi*. Nevertheless, break the kola. I give you the power to break it."

Kai kai (local/illicit gin)
They drank again and Mgbada's mother said, "*Kai kai* has a way of attracting people, so put away the bottle…"

Anara (This is similar to the eggplant, but smaller in size. In Igbo tradition, kola nut and anara are usually presented to visitors as a mark of welcome.)
"Ewo-o, my neighbor, I have not cooked. I have *anara*."
"I can eat *anara*."

Ise (Amen)
My people, here is kola nut
Brought by our in-laws
Our in-laws,
To your health,
Ise.

Ada ibe m (My co/same village Daughter)
"Please, my good friend…" Mama Theresa jumped up with the agility of a thirty-year-old woman, "please, my

friend, please *adaibe m*, not here. *Ewoo*, (exclamation) who has done this? Come."

Ehee (Exclamation), ajigijim (pride)
"I have done it. Nonsense. Why should I be relegated to the background? Are all these people sitting here more important than me? Richer than me? Good. Didn't our people say that if you do not lick your lips then the harmattan (*Uguru*) will lick them for you?"

"Mama, you are right, you are right," said everybody at the high table said.

"Thank you, my children. This place befits my status and stature. Don't you see how big I am? *Ehee ajigijim*."

Wrappa (A cloth women wear around the waist.)
She re-tied her head-tie, adjusted her *wrappa (akwaa)* and was about to leave when her namesake returned.

Mbona (Thank you) eemeka (well done.)
"My brother, how do I know that they have no money to pay? I don't collect money before they are ferried across. It is when I get to the other side that they pay. By the time I knew what was happening, they had jumped out of the canoe. The so-called good ones merely said "*Mbona eemeka*." I asked them: "Will I eat *thank you*?" They laughed at me and went their way."

Umummo (Spirits)
"You know that little children can see our ancestors in the form of spirits. That is why they are called spirits, *umummo*. Sometimes you see a child playing in the sand, and she begins to address people you do not see; but she sees them.

AkwukwoUziza (leaves), Mkpuru uziza (seeds)
Mgbada's mother was busy preparing pepper soup made with *uziza* for Akpe.

Ariba (Local semolina or wheat) (Nnii oka or Oka, or Azu iji)
"You will not eat them. Don't you know that there is famine, eh? Don't you see the way I am peeling the yam? I am going to use the peels for *ariba*. Do you hear?"

George (Imported fabric)
"She does not go to the market at all. Lawrence forbids her to go to market. If a piece of *george* costs two pounds, he buys it for his wife."

"You mean it?

"It is true, when I was dealing in *george*, any time I had a new design, I took it to Lawrence and he bought it for his wife."

The three mothers and their relations filled boxes with *george* materials, jewelry of all kinds, especially coral beads and agate stones.

Di (Husband) bu (is) nma (good) ogori (wife)
"You are no exception, *di bunmaogori*, the beauty of a damsel is recognized only when she has a husband. So, swallow your pride and go back to your husband."

Ndi (People), afia (market), (market people)
"Cook, buy our fish," said Ekecha.
"How much?"
"That's more like it; *ndiafia* how much?"
"Six pounds."

Bia (Come), zuru (buy), niazu (fish), ego nioo (money)
"These children… So, it is not time for them to go home? What are they selling?" The shrill voices of the hawkers were getting louder and louder. It was now obvious to Mgbeke that the hawkers aimed at her, for their voices could be heard clearly by now." "You children, please leave. Go home. It is late. This is not the market place." The children did not heed Mgbeke. They sang away: "*Biazuruniazu ego nioo.*"

Buru (Put/carry), agbadanti (large ear), riamaa (cry to public), Utita (local tray)
"Mgbeke shouted back if they sent you to me this evening, tell them—those who sent you—that you did not see me. "How much do you sell your fish?" asked Mgbeke's son.

Mgbeke held her breath, and suddenly it happened. The little girl who carried the basin that was supposed to contain the fish emptied the rubbish in the basin on the little boy, saying: *"Buru agbadanti riamaa."* Her task performed, she fled with her basin and *utita*. Her companions had fled before her. Mgbeke's son burst into tears. Mgbeke rushed out of the kitchen.

"Biazuruniazu ego nioo" The children continued to sing.

Tufia (God forbid), umu (children), ojoo (bad)
"And where were you when those children were selling their mumps?" "Don't worry about that. What happened?" She narrated the story again.

"Tufia, umuojoo. Where did they get mumps? Didn't their parents tell them that these things are no longer done in this way?"

Dogonyaro (A Neem tree or leaves)
"I treated her for malaria. I gathered the plants, roots and leaves of pawpaw, lemon grass, *dogonyaro*, guava and lime."

Iyi (Arushi/reincarnation) uwa (world)
"Mgbada did not show much surprise at what my daughter said. He continued prescribing the herbs and when he finished, he said to her, 'And when is your own

canoe coming for you'?" My daughter began to shout and protest. Mgbada asked calmly and clearly, 'And where is it'?"

"Where is what?" my daughter asked angrily.

"The stone. Your *iyiuwa*. Where is it?"

My daughter began to cry again. "You did not swallow it?" asked Mgbada.

"No. I did not."

"It seems as if Idenu's (Ona's sister) *iyiuwa* is buried in a particular fish."

"Fish?"

"Yes. And I would like her to stop eating that kind of fish."

Iboro (A sea bird)

"I know she eats very little. Does she crave special foods?"

"Yes."

"Which ones? "

"Prawns and *iboro* which she eats raw."

Ndemuo (Spiritual people), jere (go/went), omerife (new yam festival), eriwo (didn't eat), nni (food), iwe (anger), n'e we wo (they); i.e. Ancestors that came for new yam festival who didn't eat food are angry.

They fell silent. A song was heard from afar. Children of the compound were singing: "*Ndemuojereomerifeeriwonni, iwe n'e we wo*" Father and daughter burst into laughter.

Mgbada called: "Come, my children, come and sing your song for us."

Dibia (Traditional, native Igbo doctor)
We shall be objective. I don't say don't pray. I say go on and pray, while we try what the *dibia* I consulted in Ila (town) prescribed. "According to what the *dibia* told me, we have to let Ona (precious jewel) be."

Obi (A special detached house, within the premises, where the head of the family receives special guests or holds meetings.)
Mr. Sylvester could not concentrate in the market. He sold his medicines, bought more from others and sold them too. Then, rather than go home, he went to see Ona's father. Mgbada was sitting in his *obi* as usual.

One day, my daughter will find a husband. And when she does, her father will sit importantly in his *obi* to welcome his in-laws and to boast of his daughter.

Ese (A problem), Uke (A problem), Ogban'uke (A mysterious problem)
"I prescribed some sacrifices for them. The church does not know much about sacrifices, and if it does it does not want us to make use of them. There is something in our religion or tradition or custom, call it what you will; we call *ese*. Your people call it *uke*, others, *ogban'uke*. It

visits everybody born of a woman. It is evil. It is beyond understanding. When it visits you, you have to make sacrifices in order to ward it off. Ese visited the woman's child so I prescribed a form of sacrifice, not medicine."

Onyenankeya no naugbooyibo (To each his own, I am in a white man's vehicle)

"Two friends, you are going to buy fish?" asked Ojoru (A hard working ferry woman who paddles a canoe across Ugwuta Lake).

"And you are ferrying people across the Lake. *Onyenankeya no naugbooyibo*."

"That's what it is. We have to live and living means struggling. I wonder when it would all end."

Craw-Craw (A skin disease that causes terrible itching. The gods do not give us more problems than we can solve.)

"The Spirit has killed me"

"No, she has not. You shall get over it.

'When the gods give us *craw-craw,* they also give us nails with which to scratch.'"

Ogwe (The remains of a boat) Ugbose (cloth for scrubbing and bathing at the lake)

"There was no one at the Lakefront. So, she undressed and waded into the water. She immersed herself in the water. It was fresh and cool. Then she went to the *ogwe*, where she scrubbed herself with a sponge using black soap."

"I did, too. I took my daughter to the Lake before cockcrow. I used the herbs prescribed and washed her thoroughly. Then I left the herbs and the sponge used on the *ogwe*, as directed. This is before she went back to the convent."

Chi (A soul, spirit, life force)
"She and her *chi* know what she is looking for in husbands. After the fifth one, one would have thought that she would stop. No. She married the sixth, a man barely out of school."

Uko (A drying oven)
"The kitchen contained just the fireplace and *uko* where she dried her fish, spices, herbs and vegetables. There was a large earthenware pot in the kitchen."

Ada buada (Daughter is Daughter), eziada (Good Daughter), Ezemiri (Water Goddess)
"Ada bu ada, ezi ada, *Ezemiri*. You look so gorgeous this morning."

Ikenga (Destiny)
"Ogbuide (Lake goddess/Lake) commanded me to tell each of you to give a goat to your ancestors and to

make a feast for the *umuada* (village daughters) in your respective villages, so that the *ikenga* you took with you to your husbands' homes would remain with you and not be taken away from you."

Agwu (An evil spirit)
"You must. You know her better than I do." "They say Ona (precious jewel) is possessed by *agwu*."

Ndanda (A small ant)
"You did well to come to me, Mgbeke and Ekecha. If I were a bad *dibia* I would ask you to bring me the heart of *ndanda*, you know *ndanda*, the smallest of all ants." The women smiled. "Only quacks demand that. Go home and live in peace with your co-wives."

About the Author

Flora Nwapa was born on January 13, 1931 in Ugwuta, Imo State, Nigeria. After graduating from University College, Ibadan, in 1957 and the University of Edinburgh, Scotland, in 1958, she returned to Nigeria and she joined the Ministry of Education in Calabar. She taught at Queen's School, Enugu from 1959 to 1961. She joined Lagos University as an Administrative Officer in 1962, where she was appointed an Assistant Registrar in 1964. At the end of the Nigerian Civil War (1966-70), Flora Nwapa Nwakuche served on the Executive Council of Eastern Nigeria from 1970-1975. In 1977 she established a printing and publishing company, Tana Press Limited.

In addition to writing and publishing, Flora Nwapa was a Visiting Professor in Creative Writing at the University of Maiduguri in 1989. She also spoke at numerous conferences in Africa, Europe and America. In 1983, she received the Nigerian National Honor of Officer of the Order of the Niger (O.O.N.) for Creative Writing and Publishing. In 1992, she received a Medal of Honor from the Governor of Owerri, Imo State. Flora Nwapa passed away on October 16, 1993 in Enugu. She is buried in Ugwuta, Nigeria. She is survived by her husband and three children.

Flora Nwapa is the Mother of Modern African Literature. She was the first internationally published African woman novelist in English (Efuru, 1966) and the first African female publisher (Tana Press, 1977). Her highly praised novels *Efuru* (1966) and *Idu* (1970) were published in the Heinemann African Writers Series in London, England. Her later novels *Never Again* (Nwamife, 1975), *One is Enough* (Tana, 1981), *Women are Different* (Tana, 1986) were initially published in Nigeria. They were later republished by Africa World Press, Inc., in the United States. Through *Never Again* (Nwamife, 1975), Flora Nwapa became the first female African writer of war novels and insightful stories about the horrors of civil war. Her last novel, *The Lake Goddess* (2017), posthumously published by Tana Press Ltd., is acclaimed as one of Nwapa's literary masterpieces, bound to become a classic.

Talented in many genres, Flora Nwapa also wrote short stories, such as *This is Lagos and Other*

Stories (Nwamife, 1971), *Wives at War and Other Stories* (Tana,1980), poems, *Cassava Song and Rice Song* (Tana, 1986), as well as plays *Conversations* (Tana, 1993) and *The First Lady* (Tana, 1993). Through her children's books, such as *Emeka—Driver's Guard* (University of London Press,1972), *Mammywater* (Tana, 1979), and *Journey to Space and Other Stories* (Tana,1980), to name only three, Flora Nwapa also told stories for young children.

Flora Nwapa is the Mother of Modern African Literature. She was the first internationally published African woman novelist in English (Efuru, 1966) and the first Anglophone African female publisher (Tana Press, 1977).

The Lake Goddess is a novel depicting Flora Nwapa's ideal womanhood in her traditional Ugwuta community and by extension the world. Flora Nwapa confers women with phenomenal authority and she builds a world around them in which they dignify and assess themselves without bounds. In this book, Flora Nwapa does great justice to womanism. This is a book everyone must read because it reflects the new paradigm of today's womanhood, which the world is adjusting to rapidly.

Ambassador Dr. Kema Chikwe Women Leadership Institute Founder and Executive Chairman, Abuja

Chinua Achebe's book, *Things Fall Apart*, gives us a view of how colonialism ravaged the culture and spirit of Africa. On the other hand, Flora Nwapa's *The Lake*

Goddess uses spirituality and culture to restore health in the world of today's society. Ogbuide heals. The Water Goddess becomes Christ-like and eventually takes her place with the celestial beings in the Lake.

Chester St. H. Mills Associate Professor Department of Arts and Humanities Southern University at New Orleans, Louisiana.

The Lake Goddess by Flora Nwapa, is an intriguing expression about the clash of cultures and faith, and the trade-offs that women make, summed up in the words of the character, Ona, "women shall not be voiceless."

Dr. Eleanor Nwadinobi, MBBS, EMA, FAAC, President, UN/NGO Widows Development Organisation (WiDO) Enugu, Nigeria

Flora Nwapa's "Womanism" recognizes, firstly, that a woman is a mother that nurtures and provides for her children. Secondly, a woman could be a wife that supports herself first, then her husband and children, if she has any. Thirdly, financial independence is the theme in Flora Nwapa's novels. A woman is financially independent whether or not she is married, single or divorced.

Uzoma Nwakuche, Esq. Tana Press Limited, CEO Oguta, Nigeria

www.ingramcontent.com/pod-product-compliance
Lightning Source LLC
LaVergne TN
LVHW041621060526
838200LV00040B/1377